Edwin E. Ghiselli received his Ph.D. from the University of California at Berkeley, where he is Professor of Psychology in the department of Psychology.

Dr. Ghiselli instituted a series of courses in business and industrial psychology and in psychological testing at the University of California. He also created a long-term research program in various phases of industrial psychology.

He has published six important books and countless research articles in psychological and business journals. Dr. Ghiselli is past president of the Business and Industrial Psychology Division of the American Psychological Association and has served on the President's Council for Industrial Safety. In 1969 he completed a study of the psychological factors bearing on the success of Italian managers; he has just finished a similar study of Japanese managers. Since 1933, Dr. Ghiselli has been a leading consultant to business, industry, and government agencies.

EXPLORATIONS IN MANAGERIAL TALENT

EXPLORATIONS
IN
MANAGERIAL TALENT

Edwin E. Ghiselli
University of California, Berkeley

GOODYEAR PUBLISHING COMPANY, INC.
Pacific Palisades, California

To Mason Haire
Friend and Colleague

PREFACE

The study presented in this book is the culmination of some twenty years of research in which I have examined the traits and abilities which play a part in managerial success. Employing a variety of means, and a number of different types of managers, I have tried to obtain a picture of that broad quality which can be termed managerial talent. In the Walter Van Dyke Memorial Lecture at the University of Michigan in 1963 I brought together my first findings, and summarized my thinking at that time about the substance of managerial talent. The research reported in this book grew out of that lecture, and, indeed, is an extension of it. Here I report the findings of the application of the device I have developed to measure various pertinent human qualities, the Self-Description Inventory, to a substantial group of managers who were specially selected so as to constitute a wide and diverse sample of American executives and administrators. I have compared their qualities, and the relationships between their qualities and their occupational success, with those of line supervisors and line workers, using the results to highlight the nature of managerial talent. I have also used this report to present my ideas about what I believe the nature of management ought to be, ideas which I believe this research documents.

In this book, the Self-Description Inventory, and the scales of the thirteen traits for which it provides measurements, are presented in detail. These scales have been refined and cross-validated over the years, and the methods utilized for this, together with the results obtained in the process, are herein given. The scale for working class affinity was developed under a different title with my former colleague, Professor Lyman W. Porter. Indeed, several of the scales which have been described in other publications have been renamed in the light of new information and new thought. I hope this presentation of the Self-Description Inventory will be useful to the many persons who have expressed interest in it, and have wished to utilize it for research purposes.

The massive increases in the size of our business and industrial firms have required increases in the number of managers who are employed to integrate and direct their activities. Great as has been the need for more managers, even greater has been the need for higher quality management; as business and industrial firms have grown in size, their problems have become disproportionately more complex. As a consequence, that which was deemed quite acceptable management just a relatively few years ago no longer suffices for dealing with matters, both internal and external, which presently face the firm.

It is, therefore, imperative that there be a greater understanding of the personal qualities which lead to effective management. For as we enhance our knowledge about the traits and abilities which underlie superior performance in executive and administrative positions, we will be better able to develop ways to select men and women for management, and to devise procedures for training them and for assessing their performance. Perhaps even more importantly, we shall gain further insight into the kinds of circumstances within the organization which foster the full utilization of the qualities of those managers who have the potentiality for excellence. The research described in this book seeks to provide some of the answers to the question of what constitutes managerial talent, and I trust that it will be helpful in this respect.

I owe a great deal to my former colleague and long-time friend, Professor Mason Haire, for the encouragement and support he has given me throughout the years I have been studying managers. A man as rich in ideas as Mason Haire can afford to be generous with them, and there is a long file of his colleagues and students, past and present, who can testify that indeed he is. In my work with managers I, too, have freely "borrowed" from his thinking. This acknowledgement of that fact is but small return for the intellectual stimulation he has given me, and most of all, for the warm and understanding friendship.

CONTENTS

4

PERSONALITY TRAITS AND MANAGERIAL TALENT   55

Self-Assurance, 57; Decisiveness, 61;
Masculinity-Femininity, 65; Maturity,
67; Working Class Affinity, 71; Comparative Contribution of Personality
Traits to Managerial Talent, 75

5

MOTIVATIONAL TRAITS AND MANAGERIAL TALENT   77

The Need for Occupational Achievement, 79; Need for Self-Actualization,
82; Need for Power, 85; Need for High
Financial Reward, 88; Need for Job
Security, 90; Comparative Contribution
of Needs to Managerial Talent, 93

6

SOME WARRANTED AND UNWARRANTED GENERALIZATIONS   95

The Relative Importance of the Various
Traits in Managerial Talent, 97; Managerial Talent in One Firm: A Case Study,
99; The Fabric of Managerial Talent,
103; Case Histories of Some Talented
and Untalented Managers, 109; The
Gifted Manager and the Organization,
114; Fine, 124

1

ORGANIZATIONS AND MANAGERS

The success of any business and industrial establishment is a function of a wide variety of factors. Some determinants of the organization's success are completely extrinsic to it, whereas others are intrinsic and are part and parcel of the very fabric of the company. The extent to which a market is available for the goods or services a firm produces, the manner and amounts it is taxed, the availability of raw materials and supplies, and the competitive situation are circumstances outside of the organization which play a part in determining whether it operates at a profit or a loss. These factors are largely, though perhaps not entirely, beyond the control of the individual firm.

There are, too, many intrinsic factors which bear upon the degree to which a firm can realize its goals. These factors are inherent in the firm, and ordinarily are matters it can do something about; such as the structure of the organization, production methods, programs for training and developing personnel, and accounting systems. One of the most important of these intrinsic factors is the talent level of those individuals who manage the firm. The management plots the firm's course and guides its activities. Furthermore, it plays a significant part in the well-being of the members of the firm. The higher the level of managerial talent to be found among its executives and administrators the more effectively will the firm operate, the more adaptable it will be in a changing world; thus, the longer its life expectancy.

This book is about managers—the executives and administrators who are responsible for the operation of our business and industrial establishments. It is an exploration of managerial talent, those traits and abilities which are important in determining the extent to which an individual will be successful in performing the many and varied functions of the manager. If the quality of managers' performance is indeed a significant factor in the economic and sociological health of the firm, then it is of paramount importance to have some understanding of the nature of the traits and abilities which determine it.

THE ORIGINS AND FOUNDATIONS
OF ORGANIZATIONS

Man is a gregarious creature and seldom chooses to run alone. In the congested modern society he has created for himself, he often likes to make a great point of seeking retirement from the busy scene, wistfully sighing for the fanciful solitude of the garden, the wilderness, the mountains. Nevertheless, the occasions when he achieves real privacy are rare, and he quite fully recognizes that he really wants such circumstances merely as intervals, and not as a permanent way of life. If he is forced to have infrequent contact with his own kind, he often moves to lessen his sense of isolation by seeking community with some surrogate—a dog, a cat, a goldfish, a canary. Clearly, association with his own kind is a most important human value.

Man recognizes that there are differences among his fellows in degree of social orientation, and every once in a while he even respects these differences. While those of his fellows who require constant social intercourse may ruffle his disposition a bit, he is likely to ease them into situations in society wherein such personal qualities are helpful. Such excessively outgoing persons are made warm-up men for television shows, encyclopedia salesmen, and airline hostesses. However, those of his fellows who are at the other end of the dimension, and are disinclined to associate extensively with their fellows, man will certainly view as peculiar, aberrant, or even ill. Man will tolerate the extrovert even though he wears on the nerves and causes endless trouble, but insists upon "readjusting" or "curing" the introvert who goes about minding his own business. Isolation is not to be tolerated, nor may the loner keep his own counsel. Man seeks the company of others, and adamantly insists that his fellows act in concourse.

But working in concert brings about problems which do not occur when people act apart and on their own. With many individuals closely assembled they get in each other's way, unless there is some planned assignment of the various tasks to the different individuals who comprise the working band. If man is to work in a group, the group must be organized, and the activities of its individual members governed so that each is allocated particular functions. By this means, the work is shared in such a manner that each makes his own special contribution to the collective effort.

Groups of men gathered together in order to mutually attain some particular productive ends are not mere aggregations, a number of unaffiliated persons assembled in the same location without a system or plan. Rather, each member of the group has an assigned task, a particular set of functions, a role. Depending upon the nature of the objectives of the group, its size, and its constitution, the roles may be few in number and kind, or they may be many and diverse. But, whatever the number of members and the number of roles, the individuals in the group perform specialized actions, and the actions of each individual member of the group must be coordinated with those of all of the others. If this were not the case, then people would be stepping on each other's toes, and the purposes of the group would never be realized. If a group is to be productive, then, it must be structured—that is, organized.

So we can say that that human institution which is termed an organization is a social group, a group wherein the individual members are differentiated one from another with respect to the functions they perform in connection with attaining the common goals, their roles being arranged or structured so that their individual actions will be integrated into a total concerted effort. An organization may be a large and complex affair which is staffed by a substantial number of individuals whose roles are manifold and are enmeshed in an elaborate and detailed structure, or it may be a simple thing with but two or three members and an equally small number of different roles. But, whatever an organization's size and nature may be, its members have a mutual interest in, and a responsibility for, a common goal. They contribute in different ways to the consummation of that goal, and they accept the relationships among their different roles.

This is not to say that every individual in an organization perceives himself as a member of a group of individuals with structured roles, each of whom solemnly goes about engaged in his own assigned activities which he recognizes to be perhaps a small but yet an integral part of the total enterprise. The soldier pressing himself into the mud as deep as he can so as to avoid enemy fire, may have no knowledge of, much less interest in, the grand purpose his nation has in waging the terrible war. All he knows is the quite immediate and personal purpose—survival. If he feels himself to be a part of the organization which has uniformed him and placed him in battle, it is as a sort of appendage of that great amorphous institutional thing whose orders, transmitted to him by some immediate superior who is his only connection with the organization, must be carried out. If he does develop the feeling of membership in a group, it is with a group comprised of other private soldiers and their immediate superiors who share his woes and dismal circumstances. To such a group he may develop a firm and close affiliation. But it is not an affiliation to the massive organization which encompasses all of them.

ROLES IN ORGANIZATION

The productive organizations that modern man has constructed to aid him in satisfying his basic needs, the business and industrial establishments, have tended to grow in size until it is impossible for them to operate in as simple a way as a hunting band. As a consequence, the operations of such organizations are fractionated into parts, and to the different parts different functions are assigned. A broad distinction can be drawn between those functions which directly and immediately result in the production of goods and services, and those functions which are of a planful, integrative, and directive sort. The individuals who perform the former are termed line workers, and those who are engaged in the latter are termed managers. Line workers directly produce goods and services, or perform activities that are immediately involved in the production of such. On the one hand, there are assemblers, machinists, beauticians, and bus operators who produce things which are used or consumed, or provide services which others utilize; and on the other hand, there are clerks, repairmen, teamsters, and salesmen, who, in one way or another, facilitate the production of goods and services, or the transfer of them to the consumer.

The other class of personnel, the managers, do not themselves produce; rather, they govern the organization and control its operations. While the functions which managers perform are necessary for the productive process, they themselves do not directly and immediately participate in it. The management of an organization includes foremen, department heads, staff officers, plant managers, vice presidents, and the like. They are people who arrange things and circulate information within the organization so as to facilitate the total productive endeavor.

With the forward march of that circumstance which he chooses to call civilization, the organizations which man has fashioned to accomplish his various purposes have steadily grown larger and larger. It is the very nature of the case that the larger and larger organizations become, the more and more elaborate their structure tends to be.

Simple systems suffice when the organization is small, for then objectives are both unpretentious and straightforward. Consequently, role assignments are readily accomplished, and they are quite flexible and easily interchangeable. By the very smallness of their number, it is easy for the members to avoid interfering with each other's activities. But in large organizations, such as the immense business and industrial establishments which are so typical of our times, the task is much more difficult. The sheer geographical distribution of its members alone defeats easy communication among them. Therefore, unless role assignments are highly structured, clear and unequivocal, all is confusion. No one knows who is, or should be, doing what, and why.

All organizations, regardless of their purpose, nature, or size, must continuously provide for the coordination of the activities of the individual members so that they do not get in each other's way, but rather permit each to make his appropriate contribution. Furthermore, organizations must make some provision for the formulation of the plans which guide their activities, and for procedures which effectuate such plans. In almost all organizations these functions are accomplished by persons who are assigned the role of manager. Managers direct the activities of the organization's members, they develop policies, plans, and procedures, and make explicit the purposes of the organization. Without the government provided by managers the organization would completely lose its structure, and would then regress to the primitive state of a simple assemblage of individuals. It would be impossible for such an assemblage to achieve the group's objective, for this is something that can only be accomplished by coordinated rather than individual activity, otherwise there would have been no organization in the first place.

WHO ARE MANAGERS?

It is by no means easy to determine who is a manager and who is not, for there is no single precise and universally accepted definition of what a manager is. Rather, there are many definitions, definitions which have been developed for different purposes. It is not uncommon to take management to be those persons who supervise or lead others. And so, supervision and leadership are taken to be the functions of managers. Such a definition would include not only presidents of companies as well as foremen, but also lead-men, and craftsmen who direct apprentices. Legally, neither leadmen nor craftsmen are considered managers, nor would most people consider them to be such. Indeed, the common understanding of what constitutes a manager, vague though it be, does not include either leadmen or craftsmen, for their primary function is not super-visory. Furthermore, there are many individuals whom all definitions would include among the ranks of managers, but who nonetheless would be excluded by this distinction. Legal counselors, safety engi-neers, research chemists, and market analysts may supervise no one save perhaps a secretary, and yet there would be few who could classify them other than as managers.

While supervision is unquestionably one element in the decision of whether or not to classify an individual as a manager, it is not the sole criterion. If a person supervises others he is likely to be a manager, but not necessarily. Even if supervision by informal leaders in work groups is not counted, there are those who supervise and yet are not considered to be managers. At the same time, even if a person does not supervise anyone he may nevertheless be classified as a manager because he formulates policy, and plans or develops working procedures as an aid to others who do supervise and direct.

If a dictionary is consulted, it will be found that a manager is one who manages, and that to manage is to direct, to execute, to carry out, to guide, to administer, and, interestingly enough, to cope with, to bring about by contriving, and to husband. Therefore, it could be said that a manager is one who executes and administers. While these functions do not provide precise criteria for differentiating management positions from those of other sorts, they are at least guideposts in the taxonomy of occupations, and they do differentiate those in the upper portions of the organizational hierarchy from those at the lowest level.

VARIETIES OF MANAGERIAL JOBS

Managers may be classified by the level their positions are in organizations as being upper, middle, and lower management. Those who are in the upper level of management are concerned with the statement of the objectives of the organization, the formulation of the broad plans and policies by means of which these objectives can be achieved, and with the overall government of the organization. It includes the individuals who are at the very top of the structure, such as the president and the vice presidents of a company. In very large organizations, upper management may include the men who head major operations such as giant factories and plants. At the next level are middle management whose task is to crystallize the policies and plans developed by upper management, by formulating them into specific and workable procedures. At this level are included those who head operating divisions or sections, the so-called line management, and those who are concerned with specialized activities, the so-called staff management. Among the former are to be found the superintendents and the division chiefs, and among the latter the analysts and the training directors. Finally, there are those in lower management who are charged with putting into effect the specific procedures developed by middle management. This they do by directing the activities of line workers, the men and women who actually produce the goods and services, or whose activities are directly associated with such production. At this level are found the supervisors, the head clerks, and the foremen.

Many of the persons at the lowest levels of the managerial hierarchy supervise blue-collar workers, and by the very nature of the requirements of their jobs have risen from the ranks of such workers. Because of the particular occupations they have chosen, · they have neither the special talents nor the educational background required for the higher positions in the organization. This same state of affairs is true with many white-collar supervisors, who for similar reasons cannot rise to higher levels in their firms. The significant thing about these people is that they necessarily come from line positions and they rise only to the very lowest management positions where they directly supervise workers in line positions. There are, of course, some positions in lower management from which advancement is not only possible, but indeed is anticipated. Such positions often are taken as being a testing ground that will indicate which persons have the potential for higher-level jobs.

The lowest levels of management, then, are likely to be either terminal positions or quite temporary ones. In any event, they all involve direct supervision of line workers, and direct supervision is their primary characteristic. This is not true of the other management positions. Not only are jobs at the lowest levels of management quite different in nature from the higher ones, but they also cover fewer levels, perhaps at the outside no more than two or three, and then only in very large and highly structured organizations.

.   Let us now look at those people in the upper management positions. Here, too, we find some significant characteristics. First of all, there are very few people at these levels, and they form little more than a thin crust at the top of the organizational hierarchy. As compared with middle managers, they are concerned only with the very broadest of matters. Furthermore, often they are not just managers. Many are owners, singly or in partnership. In the case of corporations, many of these individuals are members of the board of directors elected by the shareholders to look after their interests, interests which are not necessarily identical with those of the organization itself.

It is at the middle levels of management where the great bulk of persons who are generally termed managers are found. Their positions cover most of the managerial levels of the organization, those between the lower fringe of line supervisors and the top fringe of the ''brass.'' While all three levels fall within the domain of management, it is the middle-level positions that are ordinarily thought of when one talks about managers, and it is with people in these positions that we shall be concerned with here.

There is no implication that middle management positions are homogeneous, all involving precisely the same sorts of functions and requiring the same sorts of human qualities, for certainly they do not. Middle management positions distribute along a substantial range of managerial levels in the organizational hierarchy from quite high to quite low ones, and they differ markedly among themselves in duties and functions. Middle management jobs can be classified into the broad categories of line and staff, or into functional groups such as production, finance, and marketing. But these categories are of the grossest sort, and they mask the many finer distinctions which occur among management jobs.

INDIVIDUAL DIFFERENCES AMONG MANAGERS

An organization could not possibly function without its managers. Indeed, without them it would not even be an organization, a group of individuals working together in a coordinated fashion. Managers provide the executive and administrative machinery of the organization so that all of its various parts operate in conjoint harmony, the result being that the total entity functions smoothly. The better managers perform their executive and administrative duties the better the organization operates, and the poorer they perform them the poorer it operates.

There are some bus drivers who operate their vehicles with such care that not only are they involved in few accidents, but also their passengers enjoy a smooth ride. Furthermore, they keep to their schedules, and are accurate and honest with their cash. Then there are other drivers who slam their buses about so that they often collide with other objects, both animate and inanimate, and their passengers are bounced around a good deal. Their financial activities, too, leave a great deal to be desired. Similarly, there are salesmen who not only move great quantities of their company's products from its warehouse into the hands of customers, but also service their customers so very well that they keep coming back for more. But there also are other salesmen who do little by way of lessening their company's inventory, and their few customers in disgust at having their needs go unrecognized soon turn to purchasing the product elsewhere.

Just as there are differences among the ordinary folk of Attica in the goodness with which they do their appointed work, so there are differences among the denizens of Olympus in the goodness with which they do theirs. There are some managers whose planning takes into account all possible contingencies, who formulate policies that are reasonable and meaningful, and whose leadership is dynamic. Then there are their colleagues who formulate ineffective plans that leave much uncovered, who develop policies which are both insufficient and unfeasible of execution, and who deal unfairly with subordinates and give them insufficient support and direction.

The differences among managers in the goodness with which they perform their work are certainly as great as the differences in the performance among bus drivers, salesmen, or any other sort of workers. But the effect upon the organization of the way the individual manager does his job is certainly far greater than that of the individual line worker. For if a worker in a factory makes an error of judgment, it probably will affect his own production, or at the very worst the production of his department; whereas if a manager makes an error of judgment, its effects are felt throughout the organization. Similarly, if the worker's efforts are substantial, the effects are likely to be shown only on his, and perhaps his department's, record; but if a manager's efforts are substantial, the whole organization profits, and indeed, so do the now happy stockholders.

Hence, individual differences among managers is a matter of considerable consequence. It would therefore be quite important to examine the factors which underlie differences in performance—the talents of the individuals.

TALENTS AND PERFORMANCE

The differences among individuals in the goodness with which they perform their jobs result from a variety of factors; some of these factors are found in the situation, and some within the individual himself. No one can do his job well if the facilities available to him are inadequate. The salesman cannot be expected to retain his clients if his company is chronically tardy in making deliveries. The machinist cannot be expected to turn out work that is true if his lathe is worn and out of center. And the advertising manager cannot be expected to command much of the public's attention to his company's goods and services if the budget allocated to him is small.

At the same time, the qualities the individual possesses also are of importance. Given equal productive facilities and market conditions, the salesman with the greatest degree of initiative and drive will sell the most. Given equally good equipment, the machinist with the keenest sense of form and size will turn out the most precise pieces. And given equal budgets, the advertising manager with the greatest creativity will develop the program of publicity which will have the greatest impact. Indeed, it is likely that the more talented individual will be able to overcome unfavorable working conditions to a greater extent than will the less talented one. The good salesman will have the insight and intellect to discover where the blocks to production are in the plant. The good machinist will have the mechanical ability to know where the defect in his lathe is so that it can be quickly repaired. And the good advertising manager will be innovative enough so that even with a slim budget the advertisements he creates will have considerable influence on the public's buying behavior.

One of the principle determinants of job performance, then, is the individual's talents. It makes little difference what the nature of the job is; be it a simple or a complex one, certain abilities and traits are involved in its performance, and the individual who possesses these traits and abilities to a high degree does it better than one who possesses them to a lesser degree. With jobs of considerable importance, such as managerial jobs, the role of the individual's talents is, as we have seen, a matter of considerable moment. Therefore, some understanding of the nature of managerial talent, too, is a matter of importance.

WHAT DO MANAGERS DO?

If we are going to talk about managerial talent and the effectiveness with which managers do their jobs, we ought to have some idea what it is that managers do. At least we ought to have some general overview of the managerial job to remind ourselves of the broad spectrum of their activities.

It is always difficult, and perhaps it is even impossible, to give a complete and accurate description of the duties and responsibilities of a job. First, even the simplest of jobs requires the individual to do a variety of different things. A punch press operator must see that he is fully supplied with material, that his machine is aligned, that the proper punch is placed in it, that he centers material in it, that it is kept clean, and so on. A stock clerk must check the orders submitted to him, issue material and supplies, keep a record of all transactions, keep a running inventory, order new material and supplies, and so on. Any job description which purports to be complete, obviously would require days and days to compile, and would fill a substantial volume. Second, jobs change over time. In some instances, the changes are so great that it seems like a new job rather than an old one revised, and in others the change is so small that it may pass unnoticed. But changes there are, and they are constantly occurring. Twenty years ago a carpenter very likely barely knew what a stapling gun was, while today it is one of his prime tools. Twenty years ago a vice president for operations probably never heard of a computer, while today it is one of his prime tools.

However, it is possible in a relatively few words to convey at least something of the "flavor" of a job, to selectively, but meaningfully, sample the broad domain of the duties and responsibilities that comprise it, for some of the activities connected with a job are of greater importance, and some are of lesser. The accountant not only balances the ledger, but he also sharpens pencils. The salesclerk not only uses powers of persuasion, but also dusts off her counter. The purchasing agent not only seeks prices from the widest possible selection of suppliers, but also locks his desk at the end of the day. Those who are interested in examining the content of jobs could not care less about the sharpening of pencils, the dusting of counters, and the locking of desks. But the balancing of ledgers, the use of persuasion, and the search for large numbers of suppliers are activities which the jobs were set up to accomplish, and so we would be very much interested in knowing about them. They, rather than the first set of actions, are the kind we are really interested in.

Managers perform a wide variety of different sorts of activities, and have many duties and responsibilities. Commonly, all managerial duties are not simultaneously performed by each individual manager. Rather, the case is that some executive and administrative functions are performed by certain individuals, and other functions by still other individuals. So all managers do not perform precisely the same functions. Indeed, men who are classified as being managers might be doing very different things. However, even though it is true that different sorts of activities are assigned to different specific managerial positions, it is also true that ordinarily managers circulate through a number of different executive and administrative jobs during their careers as a result of transfers and advancements. Consequently, over time each individual manager is called upon to perform quite a wide sample of the broad spectrum of managerial duties.

Students of management have prepared many lists of duties and responsibilities of executives and administrators. Quite naturally they all have a good deal in common, and by and large they present very much the same general picture as that which follows.

Managers plan. They formulate plans of all sorts, both short- and long-term plans, small and large plans, simple and complex plans. They prepare operating rules, some in the form of general policies, and others in the form of specific procedures. Managers are involved in a variety of financial functions. They prepare budgets, estimate various sorts of costs, calculate profits, and the like. They are involved in the maintenance of operations, both in the supply of materials and in the repair of equipment. Sometimes their work involves legal matters, such as contractual arrangements. The individual manager engages in a great deal of coordination, both in the integration and organization of the activities of the personnel within his own unit, as well as in the integration of the activities of his unit with those of other units. Managers are continually called upon to evaluate plans and proposals formulated by others. They are forever inspecting the operation of their own unit to be sure it is functioning properly, and sometimes they are called upon to inspect other operations. Managers perform a large number of different sorts of personnel functions. They select personnel, they evaluate the performance of others, they administer rewards and punishments, and they assign specific duties and responsibilities.

The variety and scope of activities in which managers engage can be illustrated simply by enumerating just a few of the titles they hold: pricing coordinator, supervisor of production, director of advertising, underwriter, personnel officer, comptroller, purchasing agent, assessor, market analyst, credit manager, training director, expediter, sales manager, safety engineer. It is quite apparent from the foregoing enumeration that there are striking differences among managerial jobs in terms of their content and nature. Some jobs carry great responsibility, whereas others are purely advisory. Some jobs are highly technical and specific, whereas others are quite general and broad in scope. Some jobs are enmeshed in a fabric of interpersonal relationships, whereas others are as lonely as the job of lighthouse keeper. Some jobs require extensive professional training and experience, whereas for others raw native ability suffices.

MANAGERIAL TALENT

All of this variety and specificity would seem to negate the possibility of considering an all-inclusive entity to be termed managerial talent. However, it is not, in fact, too serious a problem. When a young man first enters the lowest levels of management he is often not hired for some specific vacant position, and, indeed, he immediately becomes a candidate for a whole series of executive and administrative positions. In most instances this is not the case with people in other occupations. For example, in the trades and crafts an individual almost invariably stays in that job which he originally chooses. Throughout his career he stays an electrician, a machinist, or whatever. The same is true with the professions. A lawyer or a physician seldom strays from his vocation to another.

It is the nature of the situation that managers do not spend their entire occupational lives doing the same particular set of activities. Rather, they advance from one job to another up through the various levels of the organization that all managers take. Some take a route through one set of jobs, and others take routes through other sets of jobs. All managers' careers, then, consist of a concatenation of a whole series of executive and administrative positions, most of which are rather different, and so require somewhat different sorts of abilities and traits. However, because managers sample widely among the different jobs at one time or another during their careers, a very large proportion of them have performed a very large proportion of the many and varied managerial activities.

It is the totality of abilities and traits required by all of the various managerial jobs which constitute managerial talent. The abilities required for any particular managerial position are not completely specific and unique to it. For, clearly, there are duties and responsibilities which are similar across managerial jobs; thus, there is considerable overlap among them. Surely, then, there are some traits and abilities which are important in all executive and administrative positions.

This, indeed, is the situation in other occupations, and certainly is the case for the managerial occupation. Those men and women who have this talent to greater degrees do well as executives and administrators, and those who have it to lesser degrees do poorly in these occupational roles.

Managerial talent, then, is a broad capacity, broad in just the same way as other vocational talents such as mechanical ability and clerical ability. The jobs of automobile repairman, machinist, telephone lineman, and the like differ both in content and in requirements. Yet, we are able to group them together as the mechanical occupations and ferret out abilities and traits that are common to all of them, such as understanding mechanical principles, appreciation of spatial relationships, and manual dexterity. Similarly, jobs such as billing clerk, secretary, and bookkeeper which we say comprise the clerical occupation differ among themselves in many respects both in terms of what the people in them do, and in terms of what abilities and traits are important in the doing. Nevertheless, there are many abilities and traits such as speed of perception of details, accuracy in noting differences, and numerical facility which determine performance in all clerical jobs, hence we say constitute clerical talent. Just as there are some abilities and traits which are important in all jobs in the trades and crafts, and others which are important in all clerical jobs, so there are still other abilities and traits which are important in all managerial jobs. It is those human properties which determine the quality of performance in all executive and administrative jobs that constitute managerial talent.

Thus, a talent can be a broad human quality, perhaps made up of a number of specific abilities and traits. Nevertheless, it is a quality which plays an important part in determining the degree of success people can attain in a particular family of jobs. It is on this basis that we can proceed to examine the domain of managerial talent, the human quality which is important to success in the managerial occupation.

2

FOUNDATION
AND OVERVIEW
OF THE STUDY

We propose then, to explore that domain of abilities and traits which comprises managerial talent, hoping to learn something about those human qualities which determine the success or failure of the men and women who choose to pursue executive and administrative careers. We have seen that management is comprised of a fairly heterogeneous set of jobs, and so calls upon a broad array of personal characteristics. In view of the fact that the domain of managerial talent is such a broad one, the results of our exploration necessarily will result in far less than anything like a complete mapping. However, the insights we gain will be some addition to the growing understanding which is being obtained from the ever-increasing number of systematic inquiries into those psychological properties which have a bearing upon the capacity to perform in the job of manager.

As business and industrial organizations grow and develop, it is the very nature of the case that their integrative and coordinative functions assume a greater and greater significance. It seems to be true that for a given proportional increase in the size of an organization, it is necessary that there be an even greater proportional increase in that part of it which is concerned with its government through executive and administrative actions. In addition, there appears to be an increasing belief in the business and industrial community that by strengthening such activities as planning and assessing, the organization will function better, and these functions require still additional managerial personnel. The upshot of all this is that the number of men engaged in executive and administrative activities is quite substantially increasing year by year, and their activities are becoming more and more important.

There is an increasing realization in our industrial civilization that men should be used for the brain power they can provide, rather than for their muscle power. The increase in the proportion of employed people who are management personnel rather than line workers, and the increasing significance attributed to the role of manager, are testimony to a philosophy which holds that "work" should be done by machines, and man should be utilized for creative actions, actions of the sort he is so uniquely suited for. It is a matter of no small consequence, then, to know something about the nature of the talent which differentiates the more successful managers from those who achieve lesser success.

In this chapter we wish to set the stage for our study. First, we shall have to decide how successful and unsuccessful managers can be differentiated from each other. Unless we can do this at least reasonably well, we shall not have groups of managers distinguished on the grounds we need. Then we shall look at the sample of managers actually to be studied in order to ascertain if they are, in fact, a suitable group for our purposes. Next, we shall particularize our exploration of the domain of managerial talent, and select certain abilities and traits for examination. In conjunction with this, we ought to discuss the nature and measurement of human qualities so that we can understand what it is we are dealing with. Finally, we shall consider the instrument which we shall use in measuring the psychological properties in which we are interested.

DESCRIBING MANAGERIAL SUCCESS

If we are going to examine managerial talent, we must be prepared to indicate how successful managers can be distinguished from their less successful colleagues. The measurement of occupational success is a problem which has long plagued the social scientist who proposes to study occupational behavior, as well as those who in practical situations must concern themselves with the appraisal of the performance of workers for purposes of administrative actions and personnel decisions. It is by no means an easy task to judge the goodness of performance of those who are doing simple jobs, and the complexity of managerial jobs makes the problem seem almost insurmountable. The subject has been extensively discussed, and has been researched in numerous empirical investigations. Nevertheless, the fundamental issues have, by no means, been settled, and as a consequence there is no consensus on how job proficiency ought to be described.

Social scientists, and in particular industrial psychologists, put great value on precisely quantified appraisals of performance, appraisals based upon concrete and objective measures of all of the various aspects of the behavior involved in performance. They seek to analyze a job into all of its constituent elements, to measure each objectively, and to combine the separate measurements into a single quantitative statement, a number, which describes the totality of the individual's performance in the same manner that the geometer is able to analyze the separate dimensions of boxes into altitude, width, and breadth, and to describe the totality of a box, its volume, in a single number by means of multiplying together the boxes' magnitudes on the three dimensions.

Emphasis on objective and precise analytic measurements has put the purely subjective, overall assessments, such as superior's global judgments about the performance of their subordinates, in bad repute. Nevertheless, a very good case can be made for them. Objective measures of performance, just because they are objective and are expressed in detailed quantitative terms, may erroneously convey the impression of a high degree of accuracy and significance. But in almost every job, if not in fact in every one, there are certain aspects of performance which cannot be evaluated objectively. A typist can be evaluated in terms of the number of words she types per minute, and the proportion of mistakes she makes. However, these two indices do not completely describe her performance. The work she turns out must be neat, and neatness is a quality that cannot be objectively measured, but rather is judged subjectively. Indeed, with some jobs the entire performance can only be evaluated subjectively. For example, the performance of a receptionist is to be judged solely in terms such as the opinions about the service she renders. In some instances even though objective measurements of performance might be available, they are distorted by special circumstances so that different individuals doing the same job cannot be compared. The batting average of the pinch hitter is not comparable with that of the regular player because he is sent in only in emergency situations, when the opposition team is functioning particularly well and his team rather poorly.

Similarly, the activities of those who are charged with the executive and administrative functions in an organization are of such a nature that they cannot be completely appraised in an objective fashion. Activities such as planning, inspecting, and organizing simply are not of such a nature that they can be evaluated just by means of some objective indices. Rather, their goodness is determined in terms of the opinions of those whose activities are influenced and determined by them. While, unquestionably, some aspects of managers' performance can be measured objectively, often they are of little importance or are of little meaning, because they are distorted by circumstances. The number of people an executive confers with each day and the number of memos he writes can be precisely and objectively described, but these indices are of little consequence in gauging his proficiency in executive and administrative functions. It is often said that a manager's success can be described in terms of the profitability of that portion of the organization for which he is responsible. Even if the exactness of the required accounting procedures, which certainly is a questionable matter, be set aside, profitability is a function of many circumstances completely beyond the manager's control. Furthermore, the efforts of a very large proportion of managers, particularly those who are assigned purely administrative activity such as planning and analyzing, are not immediately and directly reflected in the profitability of the firm.

This is not to say that objective appraisals of performance are impossible, or should not be utilized. Rather, at the present time, and with people engaged in complex managerial functions and in jobs which often are not well defined, objective measures which yield precise quantitative values are difficult to achieve, and assessments which are subjective in nature and crude in the distinctions they make among individuals may serve just as well, if not even better.

Those psychologists who concern themselves with the assessment of human qualities and the evaluation of performance have examined extensively and in great detail the nature of the subjective judgments, or ratings, made by one person of another, and in general have found them wanting. It has been demonstrated over and over again that one man's assessment or rating of the performance of another is influenced by all manner of irrelevant matters. The merit ratings a foreman assigns to his subordinates may well be determined in part by whether the men are Giant or Dodger fans, and the ratings the president of a company makes of the vice presidents may be biased by whether they prefer brand X or brand Y political party. Furthermore, two individuals seldom agree perfectly in the ratings they assign to a third, and when they do collusion is suspected.

Yet the fact is that subjective appraisals of performance are not entirely based on irrelevant matters, and there is some, and often considerable, agreement among raters. Furthermore, the subjective appraisals permit not only an integration of the various aspects of the individual's performance in a meaningful way, but also permit an evaluation in terms of the demands of the setting in which the job occurs. Subjective appraisals, then, are by no means of small worth.

In our study here, we shall use subjective evaluations of managers made by their superiors to distinguish two groups—one comprised of more successful men, and one of less successful men. Certainly, as we have just seen, such evaluations are far from perfect. We can also recognize the fact that different superiors evaluating the performance of the same individual may come to somewhat different conclusions. Perhaps one may consider him to be mediocre at best, while the other views him as being outstanding. So we can grant that there are instances where the judges disagree in their appraisals. But, it should also be noted that there are far more instances where there is close agreement among judges in the assessments they make of the performance of other individuals.

THE SAMPLE OF MANAGERS

The managers whom we shall examine in this study were 306 in number. In age they ranged from twenty-six to forty-two years. Their places of employment spread geographically from Boston to Honolulu, and from Seattle to Atlanta. They were employed in ninety different business and industrial organizations. On the average there were three or four men drawn from each firm, but in some instances only one individual was drawn from a given firm. The firms included such differing enterprises as transportation, finance, insurance, manufacturing, utilities, and communications. The very large proportion of the men, some 90 percent, were college graduates, and all had some college education. Roughly one-fifth had done graduate work, in all but two cases for the MBA, and one had earned a doctorate in economics.

All of the men held some middle management position when they became subjects in our study. None of them could possibly be classified as being members of top management, and all those who were toward the top of their organizations were in small firms. On the other hand, none of the men was a line supervisor, directly supervising the activities of line workers either in the plant or in the office. This excepts, of course, the supervision of personal secretaries and the like. One other exception were the few sales managers in the sample; but the salesmen they supervised were all in the higher sales occupations, none of them being retail clerks. The managers in the study held a variety of executive and administrative positions. Some notion of the variation can be obtained by reviewing the titles of managerial positions given in the previous section, for these titles were drawn at random from those of the 306 men.

Very likely, these 306 managers do not constitute a representative sample of American executives and administrators. Nor is it likely that the ninety firms which employed them constitute a representative sample of American businesses and industries. Nevertheless, there is sufficient variation both in managers and in firms that the results we obtain from our study should have a good deal of generalizability. Certainly, studying a few managers drawn from each of many different firms is better for our purposes than studying a group of managers in each of one or two firms. Unfortunately, at the present time, the ideal of drawing many managers from each of many firms can only be a social scientist's dream.

The managers used in this study were not volunteers. In fact, they did not even know that they were participating in the research project. The test which provided our basic data was taken by them in connection with some circumstance where in they were being assessed for some administrative action such as advancement or transfer. They believed the test to be a part of the evaluation procedure, while actually it was not.

On the basis of his past performance as a manager, each of the 306 men was evaluated by another manager superior to him who knew him and his work record. In most instances, these superior officers were the managers' immediate supervisors. The judgments of these superior officers were recorded in two categories, so that the men were described as being among the more successful and the less successful managers. In the final counting it turned out that 57 percent of the managers were classified as being among the more successful executives, and 43 percent as being among the less successful ones.

We will wish to compare these managers with line supervisors and line workers. For this purpose, data comparable with that obtained on the managers have been gathered on 111 line supervisors and 238 line workers. As was the case with the managers, these line personnel were drawn from a wide assortment of business and industrial firms which were located in various parts of the country. Some of the line supervisors were employed in factories and plants, and some in offices: among them are represented both foremen and office supervisors. The line workers, too, were employed in both industrial and business organizations. About half of them were "blue-collar" workers, and the other half "white-collar" workers.

THE NATURE OF HUMAN ABILITIES AND TRAITS

Back through the long reaches of his history man has wondered about his nature, seeking some insight into the mental machinery which controls and determines his behavior. He has applied all of his powers of observation and of reasoning in seeking answers. But it has been barely a century that his psychological properties have been subject to any semblance of scientific scrutiny, and it is really only in the last few decades that more than primitive methods have been applied to its study.

It is, therefore, not surprising to find that the knowledge we have about our abilities and traits is quite limited. Indeed, even the basic nature of the dimensions of the mind are uncertain, and the amount of information about what those dimensions may be is minuscule. The examination, hence the understanding, of psychological qualities is greatly hampered because, unlike the qualities of the physical world, they are intangible. Thus, not only is it difficult to study them, but to name them and to distinguish them from each other as well.

As a consequence, there is considerable misconception about how we must regard the abilities and traits which are ascribed to man. To do this we must consider something of the theory which underlies their definition and measurement. Thus, we shall be provided with a suitable foundation for understanding the character of the abilities and traits which we shall say form managerial talent, and therefore of managerial talent itself.

Suppose a bus driver frequently collides his bus with other vehicles and with pedestrians, starts and stops his bus so quickly that his passengers often fall, and quite commonly closes the doors too soon so that not infrequently people are caught in them. We are likely to say that this driver is more accident prone than are his fellows. If a factory worker engaged in a small parts assembly grasps the parts without fumbling, places them together quickly and accurately, he would be described as possessing a high degree of manual dexterity. We note the high productivity of the crew assigned to a foreman, their low incidence of lost time, and their infrequent complaints and grievances. We would probably say that this foreman has excellent qualities of leadership.

We observe people's behavior, and from these observations draw inferences about the traits they possess. That is, we differentiate between an individual's performance on the one hand and his abilities and traits on the other, using the latter to give at least a partial explanation of the former. We say the bus driver is unsafe because he is accident prone, the factory worker productive because he possesses a high degree of manual dexterity, and the foreman successful because he has good leadership ability.

An individual's performance on a job, what he actually does, can be observed directly and measured objectively. The speed and accuracy of a typist can be determined simply by counting the number of words she types in a given amount of time, together with the number of errors she makes in typing them. We can count the number of calls a salesman makes on potential customers by following him around and watching him. So workers' performance is tangible, and the differences among them can be precisely recorded, and measured directly and objectively. But their psychological traits are quite another matter. We have seen that these human properties are arrived at by inference. From our observations of the differences among people in their performance and behavior, we deduce that there are also differences among them in the degree to which they possess various traits.

The definition and measurement of human traits is complicated by the fact that we can never observe them directly, but can only note their manifestations. For example, we can never get our hands directly on an individual's reasoning ability. Nor can we ever see, feel, smell, or hear it. Furthermore, we will not find it if we open up his head and carefully dissect away the various layers and centers of his brain. What we do observe is the way the individual behaves when he is faced with a problem which evokes his powers of reasoning. We may see him responding randomly and only by accident arriving at the correct solution, or we may observe him proceeding systematically and analytically so that the problem is solved quickly and well.

Though its manifestations are quite concrete, reasoning itself is an intangible quality. It is, in fact, what is termed an intellectual construct. A construct is that which results from the bringing together of a number of elements, a synthesizing of them into a final product. A house is a physical construct, being a synthesis of bricks, pipes, boards, nails, and the like, a fabrication designed to provide for certain aspects of people's welfare. In the same way, an intellectual construct is a synthesis, being a fabrication of ideas designed to help us understand and explain certain phenomena. The physical construct is a tangible product, whereas the intellectual construct is intangible. As there is nothing concrete about the intellectual construct, such existence as it has is within the realm of conception rather than within the world of physical phenomena. So reasoning ability is an intellectual construct, a construct we develop to aid us in understanding and explaining why some men solve their problems easily and well, while other men have great difficulty with theirs. By postulating a trait of accident-proneness we can account for the behavior of the unsafe driver. Conceiving of a trait of manual dexterity enables us to devise ways for selecting those people who are most likely to be productive small parts assemblers. On the basis of a trait of leadership we can develop procedures for training people for supervisory positions.

The traits we develop to explain human behavior, then, are intellectual constructs, conceptualizations to help us understand human behavior, and not ''real'' entities. It is, therefore, understandable why different students of psychological man differentiate different sorts of traits which are taken to underlie his activities. One student will find it convenient to separate out, name, and describe one particular set of traits, while another may find it useful to distinguish a somewhat different set of traits. Presented with the myriad sorts of behavior human beings exhibit, one student may prefer to think of them as being determined by a certain constellation of traits, and another student as being determined by another constellation.

This is not to say that each and every person finds it necessary to explain human behavior on the grounds of a set of abilities and traits which he uniquely perceives, for this is by no means the case. There is, in fact, a good deal of communality in the kinds of attributes different people think of as determining human behavior. For example, most of us find it very helpful to think in terms of such traits as intelligence, manual dexterity, numerical facility, and sociability. Very likely, there are several hundred other similar traits that we use in common parlance to describe our fellows. Quite possibly the sorts of abilities and traits we separate out are determined by our cultural heritage. We do, in fact, find that adherents to different "schools of thought" about the nature of man tend to use somewhat different vocabularies of trait names in describing the determiners of human behavior.

This does not mean that any variety of traits one dreams up provides a satisfactory taxonomy of human attributes. To be meaningful, an intellectually constructed trait must be demonstrated to have some kind of logical foundation. Otherwise it would have no substance at all, even in the realm of ideas, nor would it be useful as an explanation of machinery which underlies human behavior. Furthermore, the trait should be sufficiently well defined that some kind of device can be developed to measure it.

On the basis of our understanding of the trait we propose to measure, we develop a test which will permit its measurement. But it is absolutely essential that we offer some evidence that our test does in fact measure our trait. This is the problem of test validity, a matter which psychometricians have wrestled with for years, achieving only slightly better than indifferent success. Since abilities and traits are constructs, and, in a way, theories about the nature of the mind, there can be no single line of evidence that will be completely satisfactory proof that a particular test measures it well. Rather, it is necessary to provide a number of different lines of evidence in order to be convinced that our test is a good measure of the particular ability or trait. Indeed, the greater and more diverse the evidence we are able to offer, the more secure we can be that our test is valid, measuring the traits it purports to measure.

THE PLANS AND MEANS FOR THE EXPLORATION
OF MANAGERIAL TALENT

Clearly, there is a large number of traits which might be examined in connection with our exploration of managerial talent. However, there are many which can be excluded from consideration because they have no relationship whatsoever to success in executive and administrative positions, and therefore do not fall withing the domain of managerial talent. Dexterity of the fingers, for example, certainly has no bearing upon the proficiency managers manifest in their work, and very likely neither does keenness of smell. By the elimination of those many human qualities which have no pertinence to our problem we can substantially narrow down the list of abilities and traits to be studied.

Even if we do eliminate the many irrelevant traits, there are still a great number left—too many, in fact, to be examined in a single investigation such as this. Therefore, let us set up some rules which will provide some limits to our exploration.

First of all, let us take the position that we are interested in broad traits rather than highly specific ones. By devoting our attention to broad traits we shall be better able to draw generalizations that have some scope, and such generalizations are more likely to throw additional light upon the nature of managerial talent. Furthermore, broad generalizations should give us some insights into other problems pertaining to managers, such as their training and motivation. As a consequence, we would not consider numerical facility, for example, because it is quite a specific trait, even though it may well play a part in managerial success, for managers do deal with numbers and with quantitative concepts.

Second, let us include traits which other research has indicated are related to the degree of success attained by executives and managers. Over the years there have been a number of investigations which have turned up various human qualities which seem to fall in the domain of managerial performance.

Third, let us include some traits which those persons in business and industry frequently stress as being of significance. Cited in connection with the selection, training, and supervision of managers such traits somewhat differ from those with which psychologists generally deal. Hence, we might concern ourselves with traits like initiative and maturity. In most organizations it is held that managers ought to be self-starters and balanced individuals.

Fourth, let us select a set of traits which form a broad array of human qualities. We should not restrict our exploration to any one particular area; rather, we should look into some of the varied aspects of abilities, of personality, and of those dynamic qualities termed motivation. By this means we should obtain a better picture of the panorama of managerial talent, although we may well lose detail.

Despite applying the foregoing rules, the length of the list of traits we might consider would be formidable. Finally, the author has exercised his own biases and preferences, and in a rather cavalier fashion has cut down the number of traits to be studied to the following:

> Abilities
>> Supervisory ability
>> Intelligence
>> Initiative
> Personality traits
>> Self-assurance
>> Decisiveness
>> Masculinity-femininity
>> Working class affinity
> Motivations
>> Need for occupational status
>> Need for self-actualization
>> Need for power over others
>> Need for high financial reward
>> Need for job security

The selection of each of these thirteen traits will be justified later in the next three chapters when we describe how they are measured, and what we find out about their relationships with managerial success.

The test used in collecting the data for this study of managers needed to be short, and at the same time of such a nature that it could provide scores on the foregoing thirteen traits. It had to be short because managers' time is expensive, and often the test had to be fitted into what was an already heavy schedule of assessment procedures.

The test used in the present research was one developed a few years ago by the author, and has been successfully used in a number of studies not only of managers, but also of personnel in a wide variety of other types of occupations. It is called the *Self-Description Inventory*. The test consists of sixty-four pairs of personally descriptive adjectives. The adjectives were chosen so that both members of each pair are similar in terms of the social desirability of the human qualities they symbolize. As a consequence, in taking the test the respondent tends to be prevented from just giving a favorable description of himself, and so must project something of his actual qualities in choosing between the two alternatives. In half of the pairs the individual checks that adjective which he believes most characterizes him, both adjectives referring to socially desirable traits. In the other half of the pairs he checks the adjective he believes least characterizes him, both adjectives in these pairs referring to socially undesirable traits. The test is shown in Appendix 1.

There is no time limit set to complete the test. However, almost all people finish it well within fifteen minutes. In the administration of the test to more than two thousand individuals in a wide variety of occupations, no one required more than about twenty-five minutes, and some finished it in less than ten minutes.

From the test, thirteen scores are obtained, one for each of the above listed traits. All items in the test are not scored for any given trait, and the items that are scored for it carry different weights. The score for a scale is simply the sum of the weights of the items checked. These weights are given with the scoring keys in Appendix 2.

It would seem arrogant to presume that so short a test could possibly measure as many as thirteen different traits. And this would be quite true if we were assessing men. But we are not; rather, we are assessing traits. A test used in the assessment of men must be of sufficient length that the scores it yields are relatively uninfluenced by the effects of random factors.

In the following three sections we are going to describe the results of our explorations into the three abilities, the five personality traits, and the five motivations. In each we shall also describe specifically the development of the scales, showing how the particular items were chosen. This selection, in fact, was done empirically and not on the basis of some theoretical notions. In every instance, save one, two so-called criterion groups were selected, one consisting of individuals standing high in the trait under consideration, and the other of individuals standing low in it. The items included in the scale for that trait were those wherein the responses of the two groups were significantly different. That is, an item was taken to be a part of a scale if the "high" criterion group chose one adjective in it with greater relative frequency, and the "low" criterion group chose the other. Items were assigned weights which were proportional to the magnitude of the differences between the two groups.

In each of the following three sections we shall also provide evidence of the validity of each of the scales. That is, we shall endeavor to show that each of the scales in fact measures that trait whose name it bears. To the extent that the evidence offered is viewed as falling short of this objective, our exploration of managerial talent will be of limited value.

In view of the fact that the various scales involved different numbers of items, it is not possible to compare their scores directly. In order to do this we need to transmute the scores to some other sort of values which are comparable. Following one common procedure in psychometrics, on every scale the percentage of persons earning scores below each given score was determined. These values are termed percentile ranks and provide norms or standards for evaluating scores. Thus, if an individual's score on a scale exceeds the scores of 50 percent of the people, he is average and his percentile rank is 50. Percentile ranks higher than 50 indicate better than average scores, and those below 50 indicate scores which are poorer than average. If an individual has a percentile rank of 60 on one scale and 40 on another, it could be said that he stands relatively higher on the first scale than he does on the second.

In order to make these percentile ranks, the norms, as meaningful as possible, the test was administered to 300 employed persons, 150 men and 150 women, who were chosen so as to form reasonably good approximations to representative cross-sections of the adult male and female employed populations in the United States. The general employed-population norms for each of the scales, that is, tables for transmuting scores to percentile ranks, are given in Appendix 3. The means and standard deviations of the scores of the 300 persons are shown in Appendix 4.

Some evidence of the power of the test that we are using to differentiate individuals in terms of the thirteen traits is furnished by the extent to which the scores on these traits are related. If the scores are all closely related so that when an individual stands high on any one of the scales he also stands high on all of the others, then the test does not distinguish among the traits and consequently fails in its purpose. Table 1 gives the inter-correlations among the thirteen scores for the individuals in the sample of the general employed population, and Table 2 for the individuals in the sample of managers we are studying. It will be observed that some of the coefficients of correlation are moderately high, some are low, some are positive, and some are negative. The average of the coefficients, disregarding sign, is only of the order of 0.25. So an individual who stands high on one trait might well stand low on another. Therefore, short though the test may be, at least it is able to distinguish the thirteen traits from each other to a reasonable degree.

THE BASIS FOR JUDGING WHETHER A TRAIT IS A PART OF MANAGERIAL TALENT

If a trait is to be considered as being an aspect of managerial talent, then it must satisfy three criteria. First, it should differentiate between managers on the one hand, and line supervisors and line workers on the other. If it does not do this, then the trait could not be considered as falling within the domain of managerial talent, for it would be a trait that is possessed to the same degree by managers and line personnel. In view of the fact that line supervisors are quasi-management, they should fall between managers and line workers. Second, and perhaps of even greater importance, successful managers should possess the trait to a greater degree than do less successful managers. This is a necessary condition because men who are placed in managerial positions might have been selected for them by their organizations on the trait which is believed to be important, but is actually completely irrelevant. Finally, the relationship between the trait and success should be higher for managers than it is for line supervisors and line workers. If this were not true, then the trait would be measuring qualities required for success in all manner of jobs, and would not be just a managerial trait. If line supervisors are taken as being quasi-managerial, then perhaps for them the relationship between the trait and success should be intermediate between the relationship for managers and for line workers, and for the latter it should approximate zero.

Thus, when scores on a scale distinguish managers from line supervisors and line workers, when the scores of managers are correlated with the degree of success they attain, and when that relationship is higher than the comparable relationship for line supervisors and line workers, then we shall term the trait measured by that scale a managerial trait, and consider that it falls within the domain of managerial talent.

WHAT IS AHEAD

In the following three sections we shall define the three abilities, the five personality traits, and the five aspects of motivation, and we shall describe how they were measured. We shall also see why each was chosen as a possible element in the domain of managerial talent. Finally, we shall ascertain the extent to which each trait satisfies the three standards cited above, and can therefore be considered an aspect of managerial talent.

3

ABILITIES
AND
MANAGERIAL TALENT

In this chapter we shall examine the traits of supervisory ability, intelligence, and initiative. We shall see what each of them involves and how each has been measured for this exploration of managerial talent. On various rational grounds all three traits can be taken to be essential for managers in the performance of their duties. As we shall see, our results indicate that in fact all of them are to greater or lesser degrees related to success in managerial positions and, in addition, differentiate managers from line supervisors and line workers. Therefore, supervisory ability, intelligence, and initiative, can all be considered to be aspects of managerial talent.

SUPERVISORY ABILITY

If an organization is to function effectively its human parts must operate together in an integrated fashion, and this integration is to be achieved by the guidance and direction provided by managers. Very likely, future experience and social science research will uncover other methods which draw upon man's creativity and productive power, methods which draw upon man's considerable and generally untapped capacity for individual responsibility. However, as yet the most effective organizational machinery that Homo so-called sapiens has been able to develop to date is an authoritarian structure of individuals. In contemporary business or industrial establishments this consists of a hierarchy of individuals, a series of superiors and subordinates, ranging from the president or managing director at the top to the line workers at the bottom. In an organization, then, each person, save the individual who occupies the top spot, has his activities supervised by some other person.

The purpose of the supervisory scale is to measure the capacity to direct the work of others, and to organize and integrate their activities so that the goal of the work group can be attained. Unquestionably, the nature of the traits that are important in the supervision of the activities of subordinates varies from situation to situation, so that a person who is a good supervisor in one situation would not be equally good in another. In part, this variation arises from the fact that different situations present somewhat different problems, and so demand the utilization of somewhat different traits. In addition, different firms have different ideas about what constitutes good supervision. Supervisory practices which are quite acceptable in one firm may be frowned upon in another. Nevertheless, there certainly is some communality across situations in the capacity to direct the efforts of others, and it is these common traits that the supervisory ability scale is intended to measure.

Criterion Groups

The criterion groups for this scale were 105 persons in a variety of different establishments who were given assignments by their managements wherein they were responsible for the direct supervision of others, and 105 persons who were placed in positions where they had no supervisory responsibility whatsoever. Thus, there are compared persons who were deemed by their organizations capable of supervising the work of others and sufficiently successful at it to be retained as supervisors, with others who their organizations felt were better placed in positions wherein they did not direct the work of subordinates. The individuals comprising the two groups were closely matched for occupation, sex, and age. The distribution by occupation was 26 percent management personnel, 41 percent clerical personnel, 7 percent sales personnel, and 26 percent industrial personnel. Of the individuals in the criterion groups 77 percent were men and 23 percent were women. Those items on the Self-Description Inventory on which the supervisors and nonsupervisors responded differently to a significant degree were taken to form the supervisory ability scale.

Validity

Three lines of evidence are offered for the validity of the scale of supervisory ability. Scores on the scale should differentiate between those charged with supervisory activities and those who are not. Second, scores should differentiate among supervisors at different levels of management. Finally, scores should be related to the job success of those in supervisory positions, but not to the job success of those in positions where they have no subordinates.

If scores on the supervisory ability scale do reflect a talent for supervisory functions, then it seems probable that those individuals who are assigned such functions ought to earn higher scores on the scale than those who are not entrusted with such functions. That this in fact is the case is shown in Table 3. Here it is apparent that whether the concern is with those in managerial, office, or industrial jobs, persons who directly supervise the work of others earn higher scores than those who do not.

The data given in Table 4 show that among persons who hold management positions there is a relationship between managerial level and scores on the supervisory scale. If the scale is valid this should be the case for those who are higher in management have a much greater supervisory responsibility than do those who are lower in management. The responsibility at the higher levels may not be so direct, but certainly there is at least a responsibility for the activities of many more individuals and for the broader aspects of their work.

Finally, Table 5 shows that in the case of those persons who have responsibility for the activities of subordinates, scores on the supervisory ability scale are positively and fairly substantially related to job success, whereas for those who hold line positions involving no supervision there is little or no relationship between scores and job success. Furthermore, the data in Table 5 indicate that for those who hold higher managerial positions the validity of the supervisory ability scale is higher than it is for those who hold the lower position of line supervisor.

Supervisory Ability and Managerial Talent

The life and vigor of a business or industrial establishment lie in the individuals who people it. Unless they work together smoothly and according to a well-worked plan, the organization cannot function properly. However, to work with each other in a coordinated fashion the members of the organization need to know what it is they are to do, and what the plan is. In other words, they need guidance and direction so that they can address the proper problems, and address those problems properly. In business and industrial organizations it is the function of the supervisors to provide this guidance and direction.

We recognize the fact that all managers do not supervise the activities of others, and some of them directly supervise the activities of only a few subordinates. However, as we pointed out earlier, during their careers managers move from one type of job to another so it is probable that during some periods in their careers most of them will have the responsibility for guiding and directing the work of others. Furthermore, even if they supervise but a few subordinates, in a very large proportion of cases those subordinates, or those subordinates' subordinates, supervise substantial numbers of individuals in some operating department. So even if the direct supervision of a manager is limited to just a very few individuals, his indirect supervision may extend to hundreds. In the case of the head of a company or of a large plant, this indirect supervision may extend to thousands of persons.

Supervision, then, is part and parcel of the manager's job, and just as managers differ among themselves in their capabilities for doing other aspects of their work, so they also differ in their capabilities to guide and direct the work of those who are assigned to them in subordinate positions. It would therefore seem certain that managers would stand higher in supervisory ability than do line supervisors and line workers, and that the degree of supervisory ability managers possess would be positively related to the degree of success they achieve in their executive and administrative positions.

Let us now see what the data on our managers, and on their contrasting groups of line supervisors and line workers, show to be the actual state of affairs with respect to supervisory ability. Since the importance of supervisory ability in the job of manager is quite clear, it is perhaps needless to say that the data present no surprises. All of the relationships that ought to hold for a trait if it is to be considered as an aspect of managerial talent do in fact hold for supervisory ability.

The average scores earned by the managers, supervisors, and workers are shown in Figure 1, where the mean scores have been translated into percentile ranks for greater meaningfulness. The means and standard deviations of the scores of these three groups on all of the traits are given in Appendix 5. It is quite obvious that managers as a group are distinctly superior both to supervisors and to workers in supervisory ability. However, the difference between supervisors and workers is quite small and certainly insignificant. Nevertheless, the former stand higher than do the latter. Thus, the average scores are arranged nearly as they ought to be if supervisory ability is to be considered as being an aspect of managerial talent.

The coefficient of correlation between scores earned by managers on the supervisory ability scale and the goodness of their performance is 0.46. This relationship is pictorially represented in Figure 2, wherein on the basis of their scores managers were divided into those who had a high, an average, or a low degree of supervisory ability. This relationship is the highest that was obtained between any of the thirteen scales and managerial success. While a positive relationship was anticipated, it was not expected that it would be quite so high relative to the relationships for the other scales, thereby indicating a primary role for supervisory ability in managerial talent.

Finally, Figure 3 compares for us the magnitude of the relationships between supervisory ability and job success for managers, first-line supervisors, and line workers. The ordering and magnitudes of the coefficients of correlation are perfect, with the relationship being highest for managers, lowest for line workers, and the value for supervisors falling in between. The coefficients of correlation between scores on all traits and the job success achieved by all three groups are given in Appendix 6.

The foregoing results clearly demonstrate supervisory ability to be an aspect of managerial talent, and a very significant aspect at that. Any definition of what managerial talent is must therefore include the capacity to guide and direct the activities of others.

There is a fairly substantial relationship between supervisory ability and the job success of line supervisors, the coefficient of correlation being 0.34. In view of the fact that their prime duty is the guidance and direction of line workers, there should be a positive relationship here. The supervision they administer is not only immediate, but those supervised by a single individual generally are at least fair in number. But it would be expected that the average standing of first-line supervisors on the scale also ought to be intermediate between the standings of managers and of line workers. While it is indeed intermediate, the difference between the supervisors and the workers is so very very small that for all practical purposes it can be discounted. This is a strange state of affairs, and there is no suitable explanation.

The wide variation among the scores on the supervisory scale earned by the managers, line supervisors, and line workers (Appendix 5) shows that there is a considerable range of ability within each group. Indeed, there are many line workers who have a level of ability higher than some line supervisors and some managers. Thus, the findings also show that among those who are not assigned the responsibility of guiding and directing the activities of others, there is a considerable reservoir of talent for this function. By no means is there the lack of potential leaders in most business and industrial organizations that is so often claimed.

The finding that supervisory ability is such a significant aspect of managerial talent, a quality which plays an important role in determining the efficacy with which managers perform their executive and administrative duties, gives further substance to the ever-growing emphasis that people are the stuff of the organization. This is not to deny, because clearly it cannot be denied, that a business or industrial establishment consists of such hard things as property, material, and money. For certainly an aggregation of individuals, no matter how nicely structured and smooth the working relationships among them may be, cannot alone constitute a business or industrial firm. The physical and the financial are essential, if only to provide a place to stand and wages to pay. But the significance of supervisory ability again stresses how important to the organization is the need to integrate the activities of its members. Every organization is a people thing.

INTELLIGENCE

Intelligence, the cognitive capacity of the mind, is the psychological property of man that perhaps has been longest and most universally discussed and dissected. Ancient philosophers wondered about its nature and manifestations, and modern psychometrists have sought to analyze and to measure its every facet. In spite of all of the thought and the empirical investigation to which intelligence has been subjected, there is by no means any complete agreement of exactly what it is. While in the past this resulted in endless arguments and disputes among psychologists, today they no longer worry so much about its detailed nature and its precise definition. Very likely, in part this is due to a certain amount of sheer battle fatigue from the long and indecisive internecine wars psychologists so avidly fought about the structure and properties of intelligence. Furthermore, even though their theoretical foundations may not be entirely solid, the tests of intelligence that psychologists developed have long proven to be of considerable value in the diagnosis of personality and in the prediction of behavior.

Clearly, intelligence is a very broad domain of cognitive abilities, quite capable of being analyzed into a number of subdomains each fully worthy of being named, defined, and studied on its own merits. But there has been a good deal of value, both practical and theoretical, in dealing with a domain of general intellectual ability, broad in scope and including diverse elements, even though its bounds are far from clear and its components not completely known. At the very least, it gives an overall picture, even though a crude one, of the individual's general level of competence. Ordinarily, intelligence is considered to involve such capabilities as judgment and reasoning, and the capacity to deal with ideas, abstractions, and concepts. It includes other qualities, too, such as the ability to learn, insightfulness, and the capacity to analyze and to synthesize.

Criterion Groups

An intelligence test (the *Analysis of Relationships* test) and the Self-Description Inventory were administered to 296 employed persons. They ranged from twenty to sixty years of age, and occupationally from professional people to unskilled workers. About 70 percent of the subjects were men, and 30 percent were women. The subjects were divided into two halves on the basis of their intelligence test scores, and these two groups comprised the criterion groups for an item analysis. Those items of the inventory which differentiated the two criterion groups were scored as the intelligence scale.

Validity

The validity of the intelligence scale can be demonstrated in various ways. Obviously, the scores on the scale should be related to scores on other intelligence tests. But, additionally, if this scale is a valid measure of intelligence, then scores on it ought to be related to other variables in the same way that scores on other intelligence tests are.

Direct evidence of the degree of validity of the intelligence scale is given by the coefficients of correlation between the scores it yields and scores on other measures of intelligence. As Table 6 shows, these coefficients are quite substantial. Nevertheless, they cannot be described as being quite high. As a consequence, it would appear from this evidence that the intelligence scale is a good, but not a precise, measure of those particular traits which are measured by standard intelligence tests.

Scores on intelligence tests are positively related to grades in colleges and universities, with the coefficients ordinarily being of the order of 0.25 to 0.50. For 114 undergraduate university students the coefficient of correlation between grade point average and scores on the intelligence scale were 0.38, which is just in the middle of the expected range.

Studies of the relationship between scores on measures of intelligence and job success have shown that with those in managerial positions there is a moderate relationship between the two, with those in line supervisory positions a somewhat lower relationship, and with those in industrial jobs an even lower relationship. With clerical personnel the relationship between scores on intelligence tests and job success is about as high as it is for managers. As Table 7 shows this same pattern holds for the scores on the intelligence scale.

Finally, scores on standard intelligence tests are found to be related to occupational level. That is, those who are in the higher occupations, the managerial, sales, and clerical occupations, earn higher scores than do those in the lower occupations, the skilled, semiskilled, and unskilled industrial occupations. As may be seen from Table 8, this is also the case with scores on the intelligence scale. Therefore, these data, too, provide substantiation for the validity of the intelligence scale.

All in all, then, the scores on the intelligence scale seem to provide quite adequate indices of the level of general intellectual ability. Standard intelligence tests obviously are superior; but considering the shortness of the intelligence scale, it does seem to have adequate practical utility.

Intelligence and Managerial Talent

Half a century ago in World War I when psychological testing was in its infancy, it was noted that when soldiers were sorted out in terms of their civilian occupations, those in the higher occupations earned higher scores on intelligence tests than did those in lower occupations. Since that time, the relationship between occupational level and intelligence test scores has been repeatedly demonstrated. Men in the professions and in managerial positions earn the highest scores, followed in order by those in the supervisory, sales, and clerical occupations, and finally those in the various industrial occupations in descending order of skilled, semiskilled, and unskilled workers. There is a substantial amount of variation in scores among individuals in each of the occupational groups, so that, for example, some factory workers earn scores higher than those of some company presidents. Nevertheless, the relationship between level of occupation and measured intelligence is clear-cut and substantial.

There is, furthermore, a body of evidence which indicates a positive relationship between level of occupation and degree of correlation between job success and intelligence test scores. As we move up the level of occupations from the unskilled to the managerial, we find not only higher and higher average scores, but also a closer and closer relationship between intelligence and job success. Intelligence plays a more important role in determining success in the higher occupations than it does in the lower ones.

In still other researches, the same sort of relationships have been found to hold within management itself. Those persons who are at the higher levels of management on the average earn higher scores on intelligence tests than do those at the lower levels. Furthermore, for those persons at the higher levels there is a closer relationship between their scores and goodness of performance than there is for those at the lower levels.

Consequently, the evidence gained from a mass of empirical research shows that the greater an individual's measured intelligence, the higher he is likely to rise in the organizational hierarchy, and the greater is the probability he will be a manager, and a successful manager at that. What we know from other investigations, then, shows without question that intelligence is an aspect of managerial talent. Therefore, at the best, the findings obtained here from the application of the intelligence scale to our samples of managers, line supervisors, and line workers, can merely provide corroborative evidence for the findings of this mass of previous studies.

As is the case with other tests of intelligence, the intelligence scale differentiates our managers from the line supervisors and the line workers. The supervisors take a position between the managers and the workers, but the difference between the averages of the supervisors and the line workers is so small as to be quite insignificant. Except for the fact that the difference between the supervisors and the workers is negligible, all is as to be expected. The scores of the three groups are represented in Figure 1.

The scores our managers earned on the intelligence scale are moderately well related to their proficiency in the executive and administrative positions they hold. The relationship cannot be said to be outstanding, but it is there. It is possibly a bit lower than is generally found in other investigations, but not very much. The coefficient of correlation is 0.27, and the association is shown graphically in Figure 2.

Finally, as Figure 3 shows, the relationship between measured intelligence and success is greatest for managers, and least for line workers, so the ordering of the coefficients of correlation is as expected. However, again the difference between the supervisors and the line workers is so small that it can hardly be accepted as a real or significant difference. Indeed, the magnitudes of the coefficients of correlation for both the supervisors and the line workers are somewhat lower than other studies report.

All in all, our evidence agrees rather well with that obtained from other investigations, and gives further support to the position that intelligence is a very real aspect of managerial talent. Yet, purely on rational grounds alone, intelligence would necessarily seem to be a part of managerial talent, and the empirical evidence is just a demonstration of the obvious. The managerial job is a problem-solving job, and the problems that managers face are mostly intellectual, problems which are solved by reasoning. For example, managers synthesize ideas when they plan, and they analyze and exercise judgment when they review and evaluate the actions and suggestions of others.

Whether it be in making executive decisions, or in the coordinative activities of administration, the intellect is involved. This is not to say that reasoning, judgment, and other facets of intelligence are not called upon in other sorts of jobs, be they sales, clerical, or industrial, for most certainly they are. But they are not called upon to the same degree; furthermore, other sorts of traits, such as computational, perceptual, and manual, play a far greater part in them than they do in managerial jobs. However, let us not take the position that the managerial job is purely one of intellect, for that is not true either. We have seen that the social talent of supervisory ability plays a substantial role in it, and as we shall see later, so do some other human qualities.

INITIATIVE

There are many people who do their work well enough to meet the minimum standards of performance, who exercise adequate judgment, who are reasonably careful in what they do and in how they solve problems, and are perfectly satisfactory at interpersonal relationships when they are called for, but still are found wanting in the way in which they do their jobs. There is a certain independence and inventiveness which is lacking in their performance so that it is quite pedestrian. Such people are said to be deficient in the quality of initiative.

At best, initiative is a vague quality, and unquestionably it is a complex one. It can be said to have two aspects; one involves the beginning of actions, and the other the capacity to note and to discover new means of goal achievement. The first aspect is comprised both of the ability to act independently, and of the ability to initiate actions without stimulation and support from others. The second aspect has to do with the capacity to see courses of action and implementations that are not readily apparent to others. Both aspects have the property of being self-generative. Initiative does not imply the capacity to maintain motivation or to sustain goal-oriented activity in the face of frustration. Rather, a person who possesses a high degree of initiative is an inaugurator or originator, one who opens up new fields and who conceives of novel ways of doing things.

Criterion Groups

Undergraduate students, 324 in number and from several different colleges and universities, filled out a questionnaire in which they were asked to evaluate their objectives and motivations with respect to their occupational lives. Eight types of motivations were presented to them: the desire for job security, high financial reward, power over others, self-actualization, status, a kind and understanding superior, fame, and initiative. The motivations were presented two at a time by the method of pair comparison, and the subjects indicated which member in each pair was the most important to them in a job. By this means a ranking of the motivations was obtained for each subject. Two extreme groups were selected for the item analysis. They consisted of the 118 cases who placed initiative either first or second, and the 71 cases who placed it either sixth, seventh, or last in rank. All items on which the two criterion groups showed differences in responses were included in the initiative scale.

Validity

Validation for this scale was sought in several ways. One obvious indication of validity is the degree of relationship between initiative scores and direct ratings of initiative. In addition, certain correlates of initiative are posited, and scores on the initiative scale are examined in connection with these relationships. Since initiative scores are related to other variables in the ways hypothesized, these relationships are considered to be additional evidence of the validity of the scale.

On the basis of their work history twenty-five men who were candidates for management positions were rated on the degree of initiative they manifested. In making these ratings emphasis was given to achievements resulting from one's own activities. An individual who depended largely upon aid from others was rated low. Thus, attention was paid to the ways in which an individual obtained jobs and promotions, and to the manner in which he performed his jobs. The coefficient of correlation between scores and ratings for these cases is 0.50.

It is not unreasonable to suppose that persons achieving higher positions would in general manifest more initiative than those in lower positions. People in a wide variety of different organizations were classified into six categories in terms of the nature of their occupation. The scores of these various groups, which are given in Table 9, show that persons in higher occupations earn higher initiative scores than do those in lower occupations.

It would be expected that older persons in lower occupations would display considerably less initiative than younger persons in the same types of occupations. Persons who in their younger years manifest initiative are likely to be upgraded, thereby leaving in the lower occupations persons who on the average possess lesser degrees of initiative. Furthermore, it also appears likely that those who in their youth do possess initiative to a substantial degree but nevertheless remain in lower jobs would gradually lose their initiative through lack of opportunity to exercise it. When initiative scores were related to age, it was found that with 240 persons in management positions the older ones earned scores equal to, or slightly better than, those of younger ones. On the other hand, with 247 persons in routine jobs the average scores of older persons were substantially lower than that of younger ones. The results are shown in Figure 4.

Initiative and Managerial Talent

Managers who supervise other managers constantly deplore and bewail the absence of initiative in their subordinates, though perhaps they are less ready to rejoice in its presence. In almost every organization, stress is placed upon the need for initiative at all levels of management. It is not a quality said to be important only for positions in the higher eschelons, but is held to be equally important at the lower management jobs. It is argued that the world is dynamic, conditions change, and competition is becoming hotter and hotter. As a consequence, the individuals who are charged with the operation and the very health of the organization, its managers, must be gifted with the capacity to inaugurate changes as soon as they become necessary, and to be able and ready to develop new courses of action which are necessary to maintain the organization's prominence, to put it in a position of prominence, or, indeed, just to keep it alive.

A counter-position is advanced by some philosophers of management. It is said that initiative is required just of the few individuals who form the upper crust of the organization, those who have broad control and direction of it, and perhaps the ones directly below this celestial level. It is only the "generals," and perhaps the "colonels," who need to be the inaugurators and innovators. The people below them, even on to the "lieutenant colonels," need only follow the directions and execute the plans which come from on high. Not only is it not necessary for them to show initiative, but very likely there are few among them who have that quality anyway.

Let us see what the actual state of affairs is with respect to initiative. Do the results support the first position that initiative is important in managerial performance and therefore related to success in executive and administrative positions, or do they provide substance for the second position that initiative is not required of managers and therefore is completely uncorrelated with the degree of job success they attain?

First, we can examine Figure 1 to see how managers compare with line supervisors and line workers in initiative. From this source we learn that as a group managers stand quite high in initiative, and are clearly differentiated both from supervisors and workers. Furthermore, supervisors fall between managers and workers, and while the difference between them is not large, supervisors are unmistakably superior to workers. The ordering of the averages is just as it should be if initiative is to be considered as a management trait.

Scores on the initiative scale and the degree of success attained by our managers are positively related, the coefficient between them being 0.15. The bar chart in Figure 2 also shows this association. However, it is apparent that while the correlation between initiative and managerial performance is positive, it is at best only modest in magnitude.

Finally, we can compare the degree of relationship between scores on the initiative scale and the job success of managers, line supervisors, and line workers. The necessary information is to be found in Figure 3. The correlation between initiative and success certainly is higher for managers than it is both for supervisors and workers. Indeed, for the latter two groups there essentially is no relationship at all between initiative and success.

On the basis of these findings we can certainly say that initiative is a part of managerial talent, but we must add that it is a minor rather than a major part. There is a tendency, though perhaps not a strong one, for those managers who manifest a high degree of initiative to be judged by their organizations as being superior to their colleagues who manifest a lesser degree of that trait. So the second position advanced above which holds initiative to be unimportant is denied, and the first which says it is is supported, though by no means does initiative have quite the important role that some claim for it.

This very modest part played by initiative in managerial success doubtless will come as a surprise to many. In the minds of most modern students of organizational theory, the capacity to inaugurate and innovate is widespread, and is absolutely necessary in the work that managers do if the organization is to be successful. The considerable variation in initiative scores, as is shown in Appendix 5, affirms the first point, but the relatively low magnitude of the coefficient of correlation between the scores and managerial success denies the second. There are also other people for whom the findings will be a surprise. For there is, as we have said, a school of thought which places managers in a status not much higher than senior clerk. While it is recognized that the problems managers deal with are more complicated than those faced by the general run of clerical workers, and they therefore need somewhat higher levels of intellect, nothing creative or challenging is seen in their activities. Rather, they hold, the organization firmly discourages novel approaches, and only rewards those who plot along in a pedestrian fashion and make no waves.

COMPARATIVE CONTRIBUTION OF ABILITIES TO MANAGERIAL TALENT

Let us now evaluate the three abilities, supervisory ability, intelligence, and initiative, as managerial traits, comparing them to see which are major parts, and which are not parts at all of managerial talent. This comparison will be facilitated if we examine Figures 1, 2, and 3.

In all three traits the managers, supervisors, and workers line up in that order on the basis of their average scores, and in all three traits the managers clearly are much superior. However, in two of the traits, intelligence and initiative, the differences between supervisors and workers are so small that they can hardly be considered to be real differences.

All three traits are positively related to the success of managers, being relatively high and "highish," respectively, for supervisory ability and intelligence, and modest for initiative. In all three traits the relationship between scores and job success is highest for managers, but only in the case of supervisory ability can the required ordering of managers, supervisors, and workers be said to hold in terms of degree of association between scores and success. With both intelligence and initiative the degree of correlation is just about the same for supervisors and workers, being, in effect, zero.

Putting the entire picture together, it seems reasonable to characterize both supervisory ability and intelligence as major aspects of managerial talent. Supervisory ability would seem to play a bit more important role than does intelligence, but both are of significance. Initiative, on the other hand, must be relegated to being a minor aspect of managerial talent. Certainly, initiative is a determiner of managerial success, but not at all to the same extent as supervisory ability and intelligence.

4

PERSONALITY TRAITS
AND
MANAGERIAL TALENT

We now turn to the second area wherein there are traits which presumably might determine success in executive and administrative positions—the area of personality. Personality is such a broad and complicated aspect of human qualities that it is difficult even to subdivide it in meaningful ways so that it can be examined systematically. The traits we shall study are varied, and so sample widely throughout the spectrum of personality. Specifically, we shall see what parts, if any, are played in managerial talent by self-assurance, decisiveness, masculinity-femininity, maturity, and working class affinity. Arguments can be advanced for each as being a managerial trait, and therefore being related to success in executive and administrative activities. We shall try to define each trait so as to understand something of its nature. Then, we shall propose a way for measuring each, and we shall apply these measuring sticks to our managers, line supervisors, and line workers in order to ascertain which traits do in fact fit in the domain of managerial talent.

SELF-ASSURANCE

Self-assurance refers to the extent to which the individual perceives himself to be effective in dealing with the problems that confront him. There are some persons who see themselves as being sound in judgment and able to cope with almost any situation, whereas there are others who think of themselves as being slow to grasp things, making many mistakes, and being generally inept. The former are high in self-assurance, and the latter are low.

Self-assurance is the quality that differentiates those students who see themselves as true scholars from those who see themselves as dunces, those workmen who see themselves as craftsmen from those who see themselves as laborers, those managers who see themselves as captains (or at least first mates) of industry from those who see themselves as mere cogs in the organizational machinery, and those who see themselves as winners from those who see themselves as losers.

Unless the individual has some feeling that he can cope, he is lost even before he begins to face up to the rigors of life. Faith in oneself, then, is essential to the individual if he is to be able to act at all effectively.

Unquestionably, self-assurance is often the fool's way, leading some to tread where wiser men will not go. Nevertheless, self-assurance does provide a foundation, a support, which enables the individual to deal with the problems that confront him.

Criterion Groups

A test of self-assurance is simply one which differentiates those who believe themselves to be effective individuals from those who believe themselves to be ineffective. To the end of developing a test of this sort, several hundred statements generally descriptive of degree of adequacy of adjustment to problems of everyday life, especially occupational life, were collected from a variety of sources. The statements ranged all the way from descriptions of very effective behavior to descriptions of quite ineffective behavior. They were collected from persons in business and industry who described the actions of their associates.

The statements were edited to insure that they were generalized descriptions of performance such as "quick and thorough in picking up new ideas," and "slow but satisfactory." In order to ascertain how effective the behavior described by each item is considered to be by others, twenty-five men in business and industry rated them on a seven-point scale. A final set of twenty-five items was selected, those on which the ratings of the judges showed best agreement, and at the same time items which described all degrees of effectiveness of behavior from excellent to poor. For each item a value was obtained by averaging the ratings. In rating himself on this scale an individual simply checks those items which he believes describe him. By averaging the values of the items the individual checks, a measure is obtained of how effective a person he perceives himself.

These twenty-five items were formed into a self-rating questionnaire which was administered to 346 persons, some college students and some employed. These people ranged in age from twenty to sixty years. Approximately two-thirds of them were men, and one-third were women. An analysis of the self-ratings showed no significant differences between the various types of subjects used. The 246 cases were divided into upper and lower halves on the basis of their self-ratings and an analysis of their responses to each item in the Self-Description Inventory was performed. Those items which differentiated the two groups formed the self-assurance scale.

Validity

Validity of this scale was sought in several ways. First, the relationship between scores and another index of self-perceived effectiveness was determined. To this end twenty-one personnel officers rated themselves in terms of their individual job effectiveness on a fifteen-step rating scale. The correlation between these ratings and scale scores was 0.37.

The life histories of fourteen men applying for management positions were examined, and the men were rated for general effectiveness in dealing with personal and occupational problems. The correlation between ratings and scale scores for these cases was 0.66.

Self-assurance might be expected to be related to the level of responsibility an individual can hold. If the self-assurance scale is valid, then persons in higher management positions should earn higher scores than those in lower management positions. As may be seen in Table 10, this is the case.

Self-Assurance and Managerial Talent

When one thinks of the self-assurance of men who are placed in positions superior to other men, men who bear the responsibility for the group's enterprise, there comes to mind the military commander whose utter self-confidence, an almost arrogant belief in his own high qualities, permeates his entire troop, reassuring its members that all is well, the goal is true and good, and so impels them to great and concentrated effort and to all manner of brave deeds. Unquestionably, the self-assurance of any superior, military or otherwise, often has this effect upon subordinates. For one thing, it eliminates their worrying about outside forces, forces both physical and social, interfering with their work and their welfare. In an ever-changing and very hostile world, some measure of security is nice to have. Thus, in a business and industrial establishment when a manager functions as a supervisor, the degree of his own self-assuredness is related to the extent to which his group perceives themselves as working in a safe and stable environment. Additionally, the self-confidence on the part of the superior gives subordinates a figure to emulate. By this device, they too can approach their tasks with an assured attitude rather than a defeatism which would preordain failure. Therefore, the self-confidence of the superior may be a prod to the subordinate, impelling him to be likewise, an individual who is highly successful at his job.

Self-assurance is important for the manager in another, more direct way. By its very nature, the managerial job is one which involves taking actions. The manager is constantly confronted with a variety of problem situations, and unless he faces up to his responsibilities and takes appropriate actions immediately, the organization will just limp along in low gear. The more self-assured the individual is, the readier he is to deal with his problems and to take actions. Whenever a manager takes an action of any significance he immediately makes himself "visible" to his superiors. To be visible is risky business, for then his actions are manifest and known to his superiors, and therefore are judged by them. They could, of course, as well judge them as being unsatisfactory as satisfactory. So by taking action, the manager not only puts his present position on the line, but indeed his whole future career. Therefore, the self-confident person is more likely to be willing to sacrifice the security of obscurity and to take actions which will get on with the job of making the organization function more effectively, for he has such faith in his abilities that he believes whatever he does he will do exceedingly well, and so his actions will be fully pleasing to those on high.

After these impressive arguments justifying self-assurance as a possible managerial talent, and indeed a certain one, the empirically obtained findings are bound to be disappointing. They do indicate without question that self-assurance must be included within the domain of managerial talent. However, they also show that the contribution of self-assurance to managerial success is not an overwhelming one. On the basis of what is indicated by the findings from our managers, line supervisors, and line workers, we can only take this trait to be a secondary aspect of managerial talent. Self-assurance may be a vital thing to the noble commander in battle, but in the somewhat less bloody struggle in the business or industrial firm apparently it is not anywhere near as important to the manager.

The averages of the scores on self-assurance earned by the managers, line supervisors, and line workers are represented in Figure 5. In these presentations, it will be noted that there is the expected ordering of average scores, with managers being the highest, supervisors intermediate, and workers lowest. The difference between managers and the other two occupational groups is very, very large. On the other hand, while there is a clear difference between supervisors and workers it is not at all marked.

The relationship between the self-assurance scores and success of our managers can best be described as being quite modest. Those managers who earn high scores are more likely to be successful than those who earn low scores, but the tendency is not a strong one. The coefficient of correlation between these two factors is 0.19, and the association is represented pictorially in Figure 6.

Finally, we wish to compare the relationship between scores on the self-assurance scale and job success for managers, supervisors, and workers. The pertinent data are given in Figure 7. The required ordering holds, but the difference in the degree of relationship for the managers and the supervisors is so tiny that, in effect, it does not exist at all. Rather, it would be more proper to say that there is some relatively small relationship between self-assurance and success which is of equal degree for managers and supervisors, and there is no relationship at all for workers. At least, the relationship for managers stands out from that of workers.

DECISIVENESS

People in almost all occupations are called upon to make decisions. The president of a corporation makes decisions, and so do the sweepers in that corporation's plants. Thus, some of the decisions are of great significance, whereas others are of minor import. Not only is it true that some people are better able to make decisions than are others, but of equal, if not greater, significance are the differences among people in the way in which they make decisions. At one extreme are those who are ready, quick, and self-confident decision makers, and at the other are those who are careful and cautious, and as a consequence are slower in making decisions. The individual at the one extreme sees that a decision must be made, and goes ahead and makes it. He takes the position that it is better to make a decision than to beg the issue, that one can never ascertain all of the facts and pertinent information about the issue, and therefore action now is the better course. He argues that if one hesitates, the problems which are now minor may well turn into ones which are major. The individual at the other extreme believes it is absolutely imperative that any proposed action be considered from all angles and aspects before action is taken. He wishes to think things out in an orderly and analytic fashion beforehand, and all of this is time-consuming.

The decisiveness scale is intended to measure these two different approaches to problem-solving. Those who fall at the high end of the scale tend to decisive behavior, and those at the lower end tend to cautious behavior.

Criterion Groups

The two criterion groups consisted of persons in higher level management positions and persons in lower level management positions. The higher level managers are generally those who decide upon courses of action, while the lower level managers are those who formulate the plan of action. Presumably, the higher level managers are those who act with dispatch whereas lower level managers must be more cautious and analytical. Both groups of managers took the Self-Description Inventory, and the items which differentiated them were taken to form the decisiveness scale. An examination of the specific adjectives checked by the top managers verified the foregoing view. Higher level managers apparently view themselves as being decisive, and lower level managers think of themselves as being cautious.

Validity

A questionnaire was developed to measure attitudes of the individual toward the two different approaches to making decisions. Some typical items are:

"With which proverb do you most agree?

(1) He who hesitates is lost, (2) Haste makes waste.''
''In taking a true-false examination the best way to answer a question you are not sure of is to:
(1) trust your first judgment, (2) try to think it out.''
''You are a shoe manufacturer. The current style calls for square toes. You have a shoe with round toes which you think might sell. You decide to:
(1) market the shoe now, (2) keep it off the market for a year and watch the trend.''
The coefficient of correlation between scores on this questionnaire and scores on the decisiveness scale was 0.48 for fifty-four undergraduate students.

For each of sixty undergraduate students who were subjects in a team-work experiment, the ratio of the remarks made by the individual to his fellows concerning goal-setting ideas, directions, assignment of roles, and major suggestions for changes in procedure or ways of attacking the problem, to remarks concerning evaluation of the ideas of others, and clarification and elaboration of others' ideas, was calculated. The coefficient of correlation between these ratios and the scores on the decisiveness scale was 0.52.

If the decisiveness scale is valid, then it ought to differentiate between those in occupations which require quick and forcible action from those which rather need planning and analysis. In Table 11 this is shown to be the case for two different pairs of groups of employed persons: salesmen in the so-called ''hard sell'' occupations, where aggressiveness is necessary, earn higher scores than do those in the ''soft sell'' occupations where analysis and caution are necessary, such as the sales of office machine systems, and the sales of investments where analysis, planning, and caution are necessary. Second, men in line management positions, which involve the making of executive decisions, earn higher scores than do those in staff positions, which involve analysis and planning.

Decisiveness and Managerial Talent

The manager is frequently in a situation which calls for action, but little information is available to him on the basis of which he can make a decision. In many situations of this kind such a long time would be required to collect additional information as to be impractical. Furthermore, with many problems all of the pertinent facts just are not available. In circumstances like these one would expect the good manager to utilize his meager information the best he can and make a decision, for if he does not the operations of the organization will be held up, perhaps with serious results. His less effective colleague, on the other hand, fearful of not making a sound decision, hesitates, equivocates, and thereby may be lost.

Often, if not always, the manager is in a situation wherein he does not know the outcomes of his decisions, or only has partial or greatly delayed information. Unless he is a decisive sort of person who can make a decision and then forget about it, he never could take positive action. He would be so worried about what might happen as a result of the action he has taken that his ability to make further decisions would be seriously impaired.

Finally, in many situations almost any decision is better than none at all; without a decision the organization would come to a grinding halt because no course of action is available to it. Certainly, in many cases the kinds of alternative actions available to the manager are just about equally good so it does not make too much difference which one is chosen. After all, managers are supposed to have the background and intellect necessary to develop good solutions to problems. In situations like these the decisive manager may well achieve greater success than the cautious one.

Figure 5 shows the averages of the scores on the decisiveness scale earned by managers, line supervisors, and line workers. These presentations show that supervisors and workers are precisely the same, and the difference between managers and both of them is great, managers being far more decisive.

The association between managers' scores on the decisiveness scale and the ratings of job proficiency assigned them is described by a coefficient correlation of 0.22. The relationship is shown graphically in Figure 6. Therefore, decisiveness and performance are seen to be positively related, those managers who are decisive being more likely to be successful than those who are cautious decision makers. However, the relationship is only moderate in magnitude.

Decisiveness is most closely related to the success of managers, and least to the success of workers, with the relationship for the supervisors falling between these two. The values of the coefficients for these correlations are represented in Figure 7.

With one minor exception, the data are all as they should be for decisiveness to be considered as an aspect of managerial talent. The exception is the fact that supervisors and workers on the average earn the same scores. However, the fact that managers exceed both by so very much minimizes this exception. Thus, the factual results support our logic that decisiveness is a managerial trait; yet, it is not a trait that can be considered to be a prime aspect of managerial talent, for its association with success is only limited. We shall therefore have to consider it a secondary quality.

MASCULINITY-FEMININITY

The trait which may be termed masculinity-femininity has long been of interest. In part, this arises from the fact that it is of some significance when an individual of one sex manifests the traits, perceptions, or other qualities associated with members of the opposite sex. There are a number of qualities which tend to be associated with one sex, and their compliment with the other sex. Commonly, robustness and forcibleness are taken to be a part of masculinity, and gentleness and understanding to be a part of femininity. Furthermore, the trait of masculinity involves activity, and femininity passivity. The masculine approach to problems is said to be intellectual and logical, whereas the feminine approach is considered to be intuitive and to involve feeling and the affective. While in terms of anatomical and physiological features, men and women might be considered to be separate and distinct sorts of individuals, in the foregoing qualities those of both sexes differ greatly among themselves, and there is much, much overlap between them.

Criterion Groups

The criterion groups consisted of 100 men and 100 women ranging in age from eighteen to fifty-four years, and occupationally from semiskilled workers to professional persons. The men and women were matched exactly for age and occupation, so that any differences in the frequency with which they checked the two alternatives in the items of the Self-Description Inventory could only be attributed to difference in sex. Those items to which men and women responded differently were used to make up the masculinity-femininity scale.

Validity

The norming group for the various scales consisted of 150 men and 150 women chosen so as to give reasonable representations of the adult employed populations of men and women. The mean of the scores of the 150 men was 15.52 and the standard deviation 3.03, and the mean of the scores of the 150 women was 13.00 and the standard deviation 2.95. The scores of the men, then, are higher than are those of women. Clearly on direct cross-validation this scale differentiates men from women.

Masculinity-Femininity and Managerial Talent

Those who have discussed the trait of masculinity-femininity in relation to managerial success fall into two camps, some saying that masculine traits are a part of managerial talent, and others saying that it is the feminine traits which are important here. One could, of course, take a third position to the effect that the quality termed masculinity-femininity has nothing whatsoever to do with managerial talent.

The basic argument for masculine traits is that a successful manager needs to be forceful, aggressive, and dominant. The organization is viewed not only as a competitive situation, but also as one with inertia. For an individual to be successful, and for him to make an impact upon the organization, he must be ready and willing to push hard both for himself and for his ideas. It is said that those women who are successful executives and administrators have these particular masculine properties. Those who hold this view would necessarily predict that managers would stand higher on this trait than line supervisors and line workers, and that there would be a positive relationship between masculinity-femininity scores and job success for managers, the relationship being lower for the other two groups.

The position that it is the feminine traits, or at least some of them, which enter into managerial talent is associated somewhat with the so-called human relations view of management. The argument here is that in the operation of the organization, the interrelationships among people, and in particular the ways in which superiors deal with their subordinates, is of paramount importance. So, in order to be successful the manager must have the capacity to understand others, and to feel for them. Since interpersonal relationships are so intangible, the quality of intuition, too, is important. Those who hold this view would expect managers to score lower on a test of masculinity-femininity than line supervisors and line workers, the correlation between scores and the success of managers to be negative, and the comparable correlation with supervisors and workers to be smaller, and perhaps even positive.

As may be seen in Figure 5, managers earn the highest or the most masculine scores, and line workers earn the lowest or most feminine scores. Line supervisors fall between the two. However, the differences among the averages are very, very small; hence, for all practical purposes must be ignored.

There is no relationship at all between the scores earned by managers on the masculinity-femininity scale and the degree of success they attain on their jobs. The numerical value of the coefficient of correlation is -0.05, which is hardly different from zero. The very slight negative trend between the scores and proficiency can be seen in Figure 6.

For all three occupational groups, managers, line supervisors, and line workers, the relationship between scores and success is very, very low, and it is negative. As may be seen in Figure 7, the coefficients of correlation are practically the same for all groups; thus, there is no trend across occupations in the magnitude of the relationship between the trait and success.

On the basis of the evidence it must therefore be concluded that the trait of masculinity-femininity plays no part whatsoever in managerial talent. Not only do the three occupational groups fail to distinguish themselves to any significant degree in the trait, but the relationships between the trait and occupational success is minuscule.

MATURITY

The term maturity ordinarily is taken to refer to that state where the processes of development are complete so that there is no further natural growth or improvement. However, the processes of change seldom stop completely at one precise time; rather, they continue at a slower and slower rate, or are modified so that they become a part of other processes. As a consequence, what is termed completeness of development is likely to be simply an arbitrary point in growth. Hence, for practical purposes, it is more useful to think of maturity in relative terms. An individual who has the characteristics of a person older than himself is said to be mature, whereas one who has the characteristics of a person younger than himself is said to be immature. Therefore, maturity is usually taken to refer to the extent to which an individual is more like those who are older than he is, rather than those who are younger than he is.

Obviously, there are a variety of human traits and characteristics which change and improve as a result of aging and of life experiences. With some traits and characteristics the large proportion of the change or improvement occurs in the early years, and with others it continues into, or largely occurs in, the adult years. As a result, in certain qualities it is quite proper to speak of maturity even among adults.

There are, of course, many different traits and abilities which are subject to the processes of maturation. The Self-Description Inventory requires the individual to describe himself, that is, to report how he perceives himself. Hence, the maturity scale in effect measures the extent to which an individual's self-image is more like that of older persons, or more like that of younger individuals.

Criterion Groups

The persons used in the development of this scale consisted of 846 men ranging in age from eighteen to sixty-seven. Only men who had completed at least one year of college were included. This restriction was imposed in order to maintain some reasonable degree of comparability of individuals at different ages. Occupationally, the men in the criterion groups ranged from skilled workers to top management, with those at the youngest levels being largely college students. Those items to which older and younger men responded differently formed the scale.

The scores developed from the items which differentiate older from younger persons do not describe maturity but only age. Those persons who earn higher scores are simply older than those who earn lower scores, but by our definition are not necessarily more mature. The raw, untreated scores, then, do not measure maturity but only age. For example, consider two men who have exactly the same raw score, one man being younger and the other older. If the score of the young man is higher than the average score of people of his age, and the score of the older man is lower than the average score of people of his age, then, relatively speaking, the younger person is mature and the older one immature. This is because the raw score of the younger man is like that of people older than he is, and the raw score of the older man is like that of people younger than he is.

Therefore, the raw score an individual earns must be referenced to the average score of persons of his age so as to obtain an indication of his degree of maturity. In order to do this, for each age group the mean and standard deviation of the raw scores were determined for the above-mentioned 846 men. Smooth curves were fitted through these empirically determined values, and from these curves were read values for the mean and standard deviation of each age. From these values relative maturity scores with a mean of fifty and a standard deviation of ten were developed for each age. In Appendix 7 is a figure which enables one to transmute raw scores to relative maturity scores. It is the relative maturity scores with which we shall deal in the analysis of our data.

Validity

Figure 8 shows the means of the raw scores for the various age groups of the individuals who formed the criterion group. It will be seen that with increasing age raw scores increase to about the fifties. Also shown in the graph are the means of the raw scores by age for a group of 231 employed men, none of whom had any college education, and the means of the raw scores by age of 101 employed women, some of whom had a college education. For both of these groups the trend in raw scores is very similar to that of the criterion group, especially at the younger ages. Consequently, scores on the maturity scale are related to age for groups quite different from the original group on which the scale was developed; hence, they can be considered to be at least reasonably valid.

Maturity and Managerial Talent

In instructions to those of its officers who recruit, assess, and select men and women for management positions, firm after firm stresses the need for mature persons. In part, what they seem to be asking for are individuals who possess balanced personalities. But more than that, they want as managers people who will approach problems in a calm and even fashion. Neither brashness nor timidity is wanted. Stability is emphasized, along with a smoothness of manner, particularly in interpersonal relationships. Also involved is a willingness to accept things as they are and for what they are, but there is no implication that creativeness, initiative, and drive should be minimized. It would be expected that the manager would be forcible and systematic in pushing his ideas, but without the awkward crusading actions of the young. Essentially, what business and industry want as managers, then, are people whose rough edges have been smoothed off, and people who can roll with the punches. These are said to be the qualities manifested by individuals who are mature. If this is the image those who evaluate the performance of personnel in the organization have of effective managers, then maturity is an aspect of managerial talent.

When we examine the data obtained from the application of the maturity scale to our managers, line supervisors, and line workers, we find no support whatsoever for the proposition that maturity is an aspect of managerial talent. Indeed, there is not even the slightest suggestion that maturity plays any part at all.

The averages of the scores of our three groups are shown in Figure 5. Managers and supervisors have practically the same scores and are both somewhat above average, tending to be more mature than the average individual, and superior to line workers.

There is no relationship between the maturity scores of managers and their success in performing executive and managerial functions. This may be seen in Figure 6. The numerical value of the coefficient of correlation between maturity and success is -0.03.

Finally, the ordering of managers, supervisors, and workers in terms of magnitude of the relationship between scores and job success which would be necessary if maturity were to be considered as an aspect of managerial talent, does not hold. This can be seen in Figure

7. For both managers and line workers the correlation essentially is zero, and it is very slightly higher than this for supervisors.

In spite of the fact that it is possible to make a fairly convincing argument to the effect that maturity is a trait which almost certainly falls within the domain of managerial talent, the empirically derived facts deny that it is. It is possible, of course, that the traits which are given by personnel people in business and industry as the definition of maturity are not in fact a part of it, and more appropriate measures of them might be related to managerial success. But our direct measure of maturity certainly has no pertinence for managerial talent.

WORKING CLASS AFFINITY

Because people who live or work in the same places, or in highly similar circumstances, are faced with the same sorts of problems and have common concerns, they tend to develop similar ideas and values. As a consequence, they come to perceive each other as being of the same sort, of the same class, and so there develops an homology, a kindred spirit among them, a fellowship, a mutual understanding, and a respect. Therefore, those who are of the so-called working class, the "blue-collar" workers, often have a feeling of common ties with each other. There are those persons, whatever their occupation, status, or class might be, who would prefer to be with, to work with, and to share the common problems with those of the "working class." On the other hand, there are those who, for one reason or another, would prefer not to share these things with working class people, nor do they have any positive feeling toward them. This property may be termed working class affinity, and the scale here so designated can be taken to measure something of the extent to which the individual is likely to be accepted or rejected by those of the working class as a suitable person to be associated with.

Criterion Groups

The subjects were 371 shop workers at a maintenance base of an airline. They were classified by the company as mechanics, but varied widely in the nature and degree of manual skill they used on the job. They ranged from unskilled to highly skilled workmen, and engaged in such diverse activities as disassembling engines, cleaning and inspecting used parts, reassembling engines, and testing engines. The men were divided into work groups ranging from four to thirteen workers. Sociometric selections were obtained by asking each man to name his preferred teammates in his work group. As criterion groups the 100 most popular and the 100 least popular of the total 371 men were used. The items to which the two groups responded differently to a significant degree were taken to form the working class affinity scale.

Validity

Sociometric popularity votes were obtained on 185 workers from the same maintenance base. On the basis of the number of votes they received they were divided into three groups, namely, high, medium, and low in popularity. The means and standard deviations of their scores on the working class affinity scale are given in Table 12. In this direct cross-validation study the scores on the working class affinity scale are seen to stand up.

If scores on the working class affinity scale do in fact measure the goodness with which "blue-collar" workers fit together, then groups of workers who do fit together as indicated by having high scale scores should be more effective work teams than those who do not fit together as well as indicated by their low scale scores. The foregoing 185 men were, on their jobs, actually assigned to one or another of 24 different working groups. For each group the average scale score was computed, and the coefficient of correlation between these average group scores and the productivity of the groups was 0.48. In a nonferrous metal-fabricating plant, the effectiveness of 24 working groups, each comprised of a foreman and four workers, was taken as the rating assigned to the foreman by higher management since his rating was based upon the productivity of the group. The coefficient of correlation between the average scores on the working class affinity scale and the rating was 0.42. Thus, it is apparent that when a group of working class men who are compatible with each other, as is indicated by their high scores on the working class affinity scale scores, are put together as a team their performance is substantially better than that of a group who are less compatible, as is indicated by their having lower scores.

Working Class Affinity and Managerial Talent

There seem to be two opposite sorts of notions about the role of the trait of working class affinity, or some quality like it, in managerial talent. The first, which is associated with the general notions of the human relations movement, would take it that the good manager would stand higher in the trait of working class affinity than would the poorer one. It is thought that in order to be successful not only in direct supervision, but also in dealing with manpower problems and the utilization of personnel, the manager must have some notion of how line workers think and feel, and be empathetic with them and with their views. Otherwise, he would not be able to understand them, and therefore would be unable to direct and guide their activities effectively. There is the other side of the coin also to be considered. It is argued that if a manager is not the sort of person line people believe can understand their problems and their points of view, they will be hesitant to accept him or his leadership. The result would be that the amount of effort they would be willing to put out in their jobs would be restricted, and so production would not approach its potential maximum. Since he is unable to bring his subordinates to high levels of performance, the manager would not be considered to be particularly good by his superiors.

In counter-distinction to the foregoing position is one which holds that managers not only would earn low scores on a test of working class affinity, but also that their scores would be negatively correlated with their supervisors' evaluations of their performance. One argument for this position is that values and points of view of the working class are at variance with objectives of a business and industrial organization, and, indeed, are harmful to it. So the decisions, plans, and actions of a manager who held these values and points of view would certainly be considered to be inadequate by his superiors. This political-social position is perhaps too extreme to characterize the actual state of affairs today in the United States, pitting a militant laboring class against an equally militant capitalistic class. A more moderate, though perhaps no less damaging argument, is based upon sociological notions about a society of classes. It holds that those few individuals who are at the top of the organization and set its broad policies are a class of people apart from the working class. Whether by heritage, education, or just natural tendencies, they have attitudes and modes of thinking which are different. Being in control, they can and do impose their views upon the whole organization. Consequently, a person who stands high on the quality of working class affinity, and who happens to attain a managerial job in their organization, would be regarded unfavorably and judged as being a poor manager.

The results of our investigation support the second position. They show that a *lack* of the trait of working class affinity is a part of managerial talent. It is by no means a quality which is a major aspect of managerial talent, but nevertheless it definitely is involved at least in a minor role. Whatever the explanation may be, be it the more radical political-social one or the more moderate sociological one, there is a clear tendency for those individuals who empathize with working class people, and who in turn are accepted by them, to be unlikely to enter management. If by chance they do, the probability is that they will not be successful.

As may be seen in Figure 5, managers do earn less than average scores on the working class affinity scale, and their scores are lower than either those of line supervisors or of line workers. Oddly enough, however, the scores of line workers tend to fall between those of managers and those of supervisors.

The relationship between working class affinity scores of managers and the ratings of their success is negative and low. The actual value of the coefficient of correlation is −0.17. This negative relationship is apparent in the bar chart in Figure 6, which shows the association between managers' scores on the working class affinity scale and their success.

Finally, Figure 7 provides a comparison of the degree of relationship between working class affinity scores and the measures of job proficiency of managers, line supervisors, and line workers. The correlation for managers, as we have just seen, is low and negative. But the necessary order of the coefficients of correlation does not hold, for the coefficient is very low and positive for supervisors, and slightly negative for workers. However, it would not be stretching things to say that there is no relationship at all between scores and success for these latter two groups. In this respect managers can be said to be differentiated from supervisors and workers.

COMPARATIVE CONTRIBUTION OF PERSONALITY TRAITS TO MANAGERIAL TALENT

Two of the five personality traits we examined, masculinity-femininity, and maturity, turn out to have nothing at all to do with managerial talent. These facts are readily ascertained in Figures 5, 6, and 7. The data obtained from our managers, line supervisors, and line workers on the masculinity-femininity and maturity scales fail to meet the conditions which are necessary if they are to be taken as managerial traits. First, they do not order managers, supervisors, and workers in average score; second, the scores of managers are insufficiently related to the success of their proficiency; and finally, there is not the ordering of the three occupational groups in terms of the degree of correlation between scores and job success.

Two of the remaining three personality traits, self-assurance and decisiveness, fall within the domain of managerial talent and can be considered to be major parts of it. The contribution of the trait of working class affinity, while clear and obvious, is relatively minor. Self-assurance and decisiveness, then, are more important in managerial talent than is working class affinity. Working class affinity operates in a negative way with respect to managerial talent—a low degree of it rather than a high degree is important.

Managers are far superior to line supervisors and line workers in both self-assurance and decisiveness. The two lower occupational groups, however, are just about the same in both traits. So the first requirement is at least reasonably well satisfied for these two traits. The picture is not quite so clear with working class affinity. Managers are different both from supervisors and workers, but the differences are not large. Furthermore, workers tend to fall between managers and supervisors, so that the required ordering of managers, supervisors, and workers does not hold. But at least we can say that managers on the one hand are distinguished from supervisors and workers on the other.

All three traits are related to success in executive and administrative positions, the relationship being positive for self-assurance and decisiveness, and negative for working class affinity. Furthermore, for all three traits the degree of relationship is very nearly the same, and perhaps can be described as being low, or at least "lowish."

Finally, we can compare the degree of relationships between the three traits and job success for managers, line supervisors, and line workers. To be considered as managerial traits the relationships for them should be highest for managers and lowest for workers, with the relationship for supervisors falling in between these two. While in fact this is the case for self-assurance and decisiveness, the differences between managers and supervisors are so very small that it would be more realistic to say that the two groups are the same. But at least for both traits the relationship for managers is higher than it is for line workers. In the case of working class affinity, the order of the relationships for the three occupational groups does not even approximately hold, for workers fall between managers and supervisors. Even so, the relationship for the managers is the closest.

It is perhaps a bit surprising that more of the personality traits did not turn out to be a part of managerial talent, and that the ones that did did not turn out to play a more important part in it. For certainly it is commonly believed that personality is an important aspect of managerial talent, and good logical justifications can be made for individual personality traits. At the least, it seems quite proper to include self-assurance, decisiveness, and lack of working class affinity in the domain of managerial talent, taking them as playing secondary roles in it.

5

MOTIVATIONAL TRAITS
AND
MANAGERIAL TALENT

W_e now come to the final area of traits we wish to explore in connection with managerial talent, those traits which pertain to the motivations of the individual. We are concerned here with the fuel for the engines which underlie human actions, the forces which give both impetus and direction to man's behavior. Inasmuch as they are purposive aspects of an individual's behavior, motivational traits tell us about his goals and objectives. That is, they tell us what it is that he considers to be important—his values. The motivational traits give color to man's life; they provide it with vigor and meaning.

In this section we shall look first at a rather general aspect of the dynamic human qualities, namely, the need for occupational achievement. Then we shall examine four needs which are more specific: the need for self-actualization, the need for power over others, the need for high financial reward, and the need for job security. All of these have been said to play a part in success in executive and administrative positions, and so should be aspects of managerial talent.

As we shall see, the need for occupational achievement and the need for self-actualization do in fact play a positive role in managerial talent. On the other hand, the need for job security operates in a negative way. That is, it is a lack of this need which is involved in managerial talent. Contrary to popular notions, the need for power over others and the need for high financial reward apparently do not enter at all into managerial talent.

THE NEED FOR OCCUPATIONAL ACHIEVEMENT

Whether rightly or wrongly, for good or for evil, in our thinking we order occupations from the unskilled through the semiskilled, skilled, clerical, sales, middle management, to top management and the professions. There are those individuals who consider it to be a good thing for a person to attain the upper reaches on this occupational ladder. Nevertheless, many are happy at the lower and middle ranges of the presumed order, finding the challenges and satisfactions completely to their liking, and so their occupational interests and their goals are fully satisfied. Thus, there are some individuals who are impelled to achieve appointments to high-level positions in business and industry, whereas others are not. The former need and seek the responsibility and the prestige which is associated with high position, while others are content with less by way of status and marks of success. The desire to achieve, or at least to acquire the signs of occupational achievement, may be unrelated to the motivation to perform a particular job well. The strength of an individual's need for occupational achievement should be related to goodness of performance on a job only insofar as that performance is instrumental in the achievement of the level of occupation the individual seeks.

Criterion Groups

There are a number of different sorts of criterion groups which might be used in the development of the scale for measuring the need for occupational achievement. But, perhaps the most obvious is the best, and we can use as criterion groups people differing in the occupational level they have attained. Consequently, 119 men and 50 women holding upper management and professional jobs, and 134 men and 37 women employed in semiskilled and unskilled work were utilized as criterion groups. The distribution of age in the high- and low-criterion groups was very nearly identical. Separate item analyses were performed for men and for women, and twenty items were found to significantly differentiate the responses of the two occupational groups in both sexes. It is these items which comprise the need for occupational achievement scale.

Validity

The primary evidence of validity of the scale of need for occupational achievement is given by the extent to which its scores differentiate persons holding jobs at different occupational levels. The data given in Table 13 indicate that the need for occupational achievement scores does this quite well for the major occupational groups.

If the scale of need for occupational achievement is valid, then the relationships between scores in higher occupations should be positive, whereas those in lower occupations should be negative, for high scores indicate a desire for high occupations, and low scores a desire for low occupations. In the managerial occupations, success to some degree in part is gauged by the degree to which the individual is challenged by executive and administrative duties to the extent that he is impelled to move ahead to higher levels. On the other hand, those who are employed in the lower, and in particular the industrial occupations, are valued only insofar as they perform the tasks prescribed. Those who are ambitious to seek positions higher in the occupational scale are likely to be regarded as not being primarily concerned with their jobs, and consequently are considered to be less desirable workers. That these relationships do in fact hold for the need for occupational achievement scale is demonstrated by the data shown in Table 14.

Need for Occupational Status and Managerial Talent

One popular notion about managers is that they are people who are ambitious, ambitious in the sense that they are impelled to seek high positions in their organizations. Furthermore, those managers who perform their executive and administrative functions exceptionally well are held to be even more ambitious, for it is said that they strive to outperform their colleagues in order to achieve even higher positions.

There are many reasons why an individual would wish to be upward mobile occupationally, and to set his sights on high station. Quite obviously high station provides a considerable financial reward, but it also carries a variety of other perquisites. The person who holds a high-level job has the independence necessary to carry out his ideas, and the authority to carry them out in his own way. He can exercise power over others, and has greater control over the whole situation which concerns him. At these levels the individual has a job of greater scope, challenge, and responsibility, together with greater recognition and rewards.

On the basis of the foregoing logic, it would be fully expected that the need for occupational achievement would be a significant aspect of managerial talent. It reflects a fundamental desire for achievement, and for the opportunity to accomplish it.

The averages of the scores earned by managers, supervisors, and workers on the scale designed to measure the need for occupational achievement are shown in Figure 9. The figure clearly shows that there is a marked difference among the three occupational groups in their average scores, and that their order in terms of average scores is just what would be expected if this need is to be considered as falling within the domain of managerial talent.

As may be seen in Figure 10, there is a very substantial degree of relationship between the scores managers earn on the scale of need for occupational achievement and the extent to which they are able to achieve success as executives and administrators. Those who earn the higher scores are much more likely to be successful than are those who earn lower scores. The coefficient of correlation is 0.34.

Finally, Figure 11 demonstrates the fact that the required order of the three occupational groups holds for the relationship between need scores and job success. The correlation is highest for managers and lowest for workers, with supervisors falling between these two. The difference between managers and supervisors is quite large, but while supervisors do fall above workers, the difference between them actually is so small as to be discounted.

All in all, it seems quite clear not only that the need for occupational achievement necessarily must be considered to be a part of managerial talent, but also that it is a most important part. Those who seek entry into management, and those who achieve the greatest degree of success in it, have a strong desire to achieve high position.

NEED FOR SELF-ACTUALIZATION

Some people need, and therefore seek, the opportunity to utilize their talents to the fullest extent. They wish to be creative through the exercise of their own capabilities, and they feel strongly that those capabilities must not be left unfulfilled, but rather must be made manifest in concrete actions. For them, self-actualization is of paramount importance. Furthermore, their motivation is such that they must utilize their talents in something they believe to be worthwhile, in an activity which is important, and in which achievement is of consequence to society. Other individuals seem to be perfectly willing to work at jobs which do not demand of them the full exercise of their talents. They have no particular desire to realize their potentialities, to draw upon their personal qualities to the utmost. What satisfactions they do get from their work are not those which come from the use of their personal qualities, but rather from sources outside of themselves, principally in the form of tangible rewards rather than in personal satisfactions. They are not necessarily unmotivated to achieve success; indeed, in many instances their desire for tangible rewards may even be stronger than that of persons of the first sort. The scale for the measurement of the strength of the need for self-actualization is intended to provide an indication of the extent to which the individual needs and wants to utilize his talents to the fullest.

Criterion Groups

Undergraduate students, 313 in number, filled out the questionnaire on objectives and motivations mentioned previously in connection with the initiative scale. The students were divided into the approximate half who reported that they had a strong need for self-actualization, and those who stated that for them the need was less important than other needs. The items which differentiated these two criterion groups formed the self-actualization scale.

Validity

Interviews pertaining to their careers were conducted with 170 men who were employed either in managerial or in higher sales occupations. Information was obtained from them with respect to why they chose certain paths rather than others, why they sought certain types of jobs, and how they reacted to, and performed on, the various jobs they held. On the basis of this information they were rated in terms of the strength of their need for self-actualization, that is, the extent to which they wanted to utilize their capacities to the fullest in work that they considered to be of significance both to themselves and to society. In spite of the fact that they were all superior people and therefore quite homogeneous, the relationship between the ratings and the scores they earned on the need for self-actualization scale was by no means insignificant, the coefficient of correlation being 0.41.

Need for Self-Actualization and Managerial Talent

A view advanced some years ago, and still firmly supported today in certain circles, holds that managers are completely establishment oriented. This notion has been embodied in the phrase "organization man." Essentially, it is claimed that managers are compliers, and must do things the "company way" if they are just to hold on to their very positions, much less if they are to advance in their firms. The position taken is that the managers who are well regarded by their supervisors are those who do their assigned work precisely in the manner prescribed, and without variance from accustomed modes. The implication is that they operate in a completely pedestrian fashion, doing precisely what they are supposed to, and no more and no less. Uniqueness is to be avoided, one must never make waves, and stereotopy of behavior and of attitudes is the rule.

Very likely this notion is not completely without some measure of validity. It seems quite probable that the foregoing does in fact well describe the state of affairs in some firms, particularly those which have become institutionalized and static. Nevertheless, contemporary philosophers of organizational matters argue just the opposite. They stress the importance of creativity at the managerial level, insisting that business and industrial organizations must foster self-actualization among their executives and administrators, and the originality and individuality that goes along with it. Indeed, the general tenor of the empirical evidence on the subject does seem to indicate that successful managers are those who are able to utilize their capabilities to the fullest in activities they regard as being significant.

In Figure 9 we find the averages of the scores of managers, supervisors, and workers on the scale designed to measure the strength of the need for self-actualization. It is quite apparent from these presentations of the data that the expected ordering of the three occupations holds, managers earning the highest scores and workers the lowest, with supervisors falling in between them. Indeed, the difference between managers and supervisors is far greater than is the difference between supervisors and workers.

The coefficient of correlation between success and the scores the managers in our sample earned on the self-actualization scale is 0.26. The positive relationship is shown graphically in Figure 10. It is apparent that there is a significant degree of association between self-actualization and managerial success. Those managers who earn the higher scores on the self-actualization scale are much more likely to be successful than are those who earn lower scores.

Finally, Figure 11 compares the degree of relationship between self-actualization scores and success for managers, supervisors and workers. The expected ordering of the correlations does not precisely hold here. While managers are differentiated from supervisors and workers, the relationship for the latter two groups are just about the same. The relationship for managers is moderately substantial and positive, but for all practical purposes there is no relationship whatsoever for either the supervisors or the workers.

The findings of the present investigation support the view that self-actualization is indeed a significant part of managerial talent. Not only are managers distinguished from supervisors and workers in terms of average scores and in degree of relationship between scores and success, but in addition, for managers the relationship between scores and success is at least moderate in magnitude. Creativity and self-realization, then, clearly play a definite part in determining who will enter management, and who will attain success in it.

NEED FOR POWER

There are some individuals who have a strong need to exercise power over their fellows. They wish and seek positions and circumstances wherein they can direct and control the activities of others. They want a unilateral command so that they have full authority and the wherewithal to enforce their will and to impose their ideas upon others. On the other hand, there are those individuals who do not wish this sort of power, and, indeed, avoid it insofar as possible. If they are thrust into positions of authority, they are likely to delegate responsibility as much as possible, and to guide the actions of others by persuasion rather than by executive order. It is not that they are unwilling to be leaders, or even that they have no strong views about what others should do or think. Rather, it is just that they have no stomach for controlling the activities of other people in a direct and absolute fashion. The scale of need for power is aimed at measuring the strength of the individual's desire for control over others.

Criterion Groups

The 313 students who filled out the objectives and motivations questionnaire were also divided into the approximate half who put their need for power as paramount, and the half who reported little or no need for power. By this means two contrasting criterion groups were formed. The items which differentiated these two groups comprised the scale designed to measure the need for power.

Validity

In general, it would be expected that managers who seek and are placed in line positions would be more highly motivated to exercise power over others than would those who are in staff positions. This appears to be the case inasmuch as 189 men in line management positions earned higher scores on the need for power scale than did 92 men in staff management positions. The average score of line managers was 12.09, and that of staff managers was only 9.51.

It would seem that the desire for power would be considered to be more important in those organizations with an authoritarian climate than in those with a democratic climate. If the climate of an establishment is authoritarian then it would be expected that a higher relationship would hold between the scores earned by supervisory personnel and the organizations' evaluation of their performance than it would be an establishment with a democratic climate. Eight business and industrial establishments were ranked in terms of the degree to which it was estimated that the management was authoritarian oriented rather than democratic oriented. In the four most authoritarian organizations the coefficients of correlation between the ratings of success of first-line supervisors and their scores on the scale for need for power were 0.36, 0.15, 0.15, and −0.15, whereas in the four least authoritarian organizations the coefficients were 0.09, 0.09, 0.05, and −0.23. This evidence is quite suggestive of the validity of the scale for need for power.

Need for Power and Managerial Talent

It would perhaps not be unreasonable to consider that the desire for power over others would be a part of managerial talent. At least for those managers who are in the so-called line positions the need for power might seem to be important, for by the very nature of their jobs they must actively supervise the activities of others, manipulating them in order to achieve the organization's goals. But it would appear that even those managers who do not have immediate supervision over any large number of subordinates would find power necessary so that they can control the direction of that portion of the organization which falls under their jurisdiction, and therefore for which they are responsible. Consequently, it would not be surprising to find that those who seek management positions, and those who achieve the greatest success in them, have a greater need for power.

However, power in the sense of being able to direct the actions of others is only one way of influencing them. Persuasion and allied means of guidance are also possibilities. Power might be the proper approach in an organization wherein the climate is an authoritarian one, but in modern business and industrial establishments, it appears that a more democratic variety of government tends to be favored. Consequently, it is quite possible that the need for power does not play any part whatsoever in managerial talent.

On the average, supervisors and workers earn exactly the same scores on the scale of power need, and the scores of managers are slightly higher. This may be seen in Figure 9, which presents the averages of the scores of the three occupational groups.

The relationship between the strength of the need for power and the level of success achieved by managers is quite low. The coefficient of correlation is only 0.03, and the association is shown graphically in Figure 10. Though the relationship is positive, for all practical purposes it is so small as to be negligible. At the best, it would have to be concluded that the relationship is very, very slight, and probably is nonexistent.

The degree of correlation between scores on the scale of need for power and job success is positive both for managers and supervisors, but in both cases the relationships are so low as to be quite unimportant. Furthermore, the relationship is higher for supervisors than it is for managers. In the case of workers, it is negative. The relevant data are presented in Figure 11.

The order of managers, supervisors, and workers does not hold in terms of average scores and in the degree of relationship between scores and success if the need for power is to be considered as being a part of managerial talent. Although, on the average, the scores of managers are superior to those of supervisors and workers, and the relationship between scores and success is different for workers than it is for managers and supervisors, the needed arrangements of them are lacking. But taking all of the evidence together, it would appear that the need for power over others has very little, if anything, to do with managerial talent.

NEED FOR HIGH FINANCIAL REWARD

Not too many years ago, it was held that man worked solely and entirely for financial gain. It was argued that he did not obtain, nor did he expect, other from his job save money, money which paid for the time and effort he gave to his job. However, during the past half-century social science research has shattered the image of economic man. It has quite clearly shown that those who labor do receive, and indeed, expect, more satisfactions from their labors than just money. As a consequence, in recent years the importance of financial reward for work has been so greatly minimized that it might seem that no one is really interested in it at all. Nevertheless, for some individuals financial reward is of utmost importance. They seek money either for itself, or for what can be bought with it. For them money is not merely a symbol of success, but rather it is something of significance in and of itself, and because it provides the wherewithal for other acquisitions. Other individuals may not be entirely happy with the amount of money they earn, but there are other needs which for them are more salient, and the satisfaction of these needs they regard as much more urgent. The purpose of the scale for measuring need for high financial reward is to provide some index of the primacy of the individual's desire for monetary gain from his work.

Criterion Groups

This scale was formed by the items which differentiated students who stated that high financial reward for itself alone was of paramount importance to them, from those who did not so regard rewards of this tangible sort. The students were the 313 mentioned before, and the basis of their division into criterion groups was their responses on the objectives and motivations questionnaire.

Validity

The 170 men holding managerial and higher sales jobs who were given the career interview were also rated for the strength of their desire to achieve high financial rewards over other sorts of rewards in their occupational pursuits. The coefficient of correlation between the ratings and scores on the scale for measuring the need for high financial reward was 0.42. Again, the fact that an association of this degree was obtained with such a homogeneous group is significant.

Need for High Financial Reward and Managerial Talent

In view of the fact that managerial positions are high in the organizational hierarchy and consequently carry higher pay, it would seem that the desire for financial reward must necessarily be associated with those qualities which constitute managerial talent. Why else, it might well be asked, would anyone seek entry into management save for the greater financial remuneration it offers, and once in it give forth with the extra effort to perform well save for the expectancy of even greater pay. Yet clearly, there are a wide variety of other sorts of rewards which are received by those holding executive and administrative jobs. These other rewards might be considered to be of greater immediate moment if the current stipend is deemed sufficient. Thus, it is quite possible that pay might not be a prime factor in determining managerial performance.

From Figure 9 the order of the three occupational groups, the managers, the line supervisors, and the line workers, in terms of average scores can be ascertained. It will be observed that the prescribed order of occupations holds, and holds exactly, but in reverse. Managers earn the lowest scores, workers the highest, and supervisors fall in between them. So high pay has greater primacy as a motivation for line workers than it has for line supervisors, and greater primacy for line supervisors than it has for managers.

The relationship between scores earned by managers on the scale of need for high financial reward and their success is rather low and negative. The coefficient of correlation between scores and success if −0.18, and the relationship is shown graphically in Figure 10. This means that those managers who have a strong need for a high financial reward are less likely to be successful, and those whose need for high financial reward is less strong are more likely to be successful.

In Figure 11 we can see the ordering of the three occupational groups in terms of the degree of association between scores on the scale measuring need for high financial reward and success. From these presentations it can be seen that the differences between the groups are small, and while the relationship for managers is different from that of supervisors and workers, the necessary ordering of occupations does not strictly hold.

The need for high financial reward satisfies some of the necessary relationships to be considered a part of managerial talent, but the relationships are generally not strong. It is also apparent that the relationships are inverse in direction. Consequently, we must say that it is a lack of the need for high financial reward that might be an aspect of managerial talent, but at best it is a borderline factor.

NEED FOR JOB SECURITY

There are many people who are always concerned about their job security, and so a large portion of their efforts and activities are directed to establishing and firming their positions in their organizations. They are fearful that they might be given unfavorable work loads or work assignments, and endeavor to protect both their jobs and their status. The possibility of unfair actions against them on the part of their superiors is one of their constant concerns. They are unsure even of the very tenure of their employment. These people can be compared with other individuals who are so confident in their own talents, and have such faith in the circumstances in which they work, that they are entirely unworried about how they will be dealt with by their organization or their superiors. Furthermore, they are unconcerned about the continuity of their employment. They have no doubt but that if their present jobs ceased to exist, or if for one reason or another they lost them, before very long they could easily find other employment that would be at least equally good. Scores of the strength of need for security presume to differentiate people in terms of the extent to which they are fearful of their circumstances and want protection from adverse forces.

Criterion Groups

Again the 313 students described before were divided into approximately two halves on the basis of their responses to the objectives and motivations questionnaire. This time the division was on the basis of whether they were or were not primarily concerned with job security. Those items which differentiate between the two groups are scored to provide a measure of need for job security.

Validity

The 170 employed men mentioned earlier who were interviewed about their careers were divided into the 60 who were judged to have a substantial need for occupational stability and job security and were unwilling to consider risky positions with potentially high financial reward, and the 110 who were considered to be less interested in security of employment and more in challenge and individual action. Those with a greater need for security obtained an average score of 10.77, and those with a lesser need for it obtained an average score of only 9.25.

Need for Job Security and Managerial Talent

Because management positions are high offices in the organization, it is not surprising to find that they are commonly considered as being secure. But this is not at all the case; in fact, those who hold executive and administrative positions ordinarily are subject to arbitrary transfer or termination, and generally have no formal recourse. People in other sorts of positions have the protection provided by unions and other similar associations. But in management the individual stands alone, and is without any powerful established machinery for assuring him the continuity of his employment and favorable conditions of work. All he can depend upon are his own powers of persuasion, and any informal alliances he might have developed with others in high places in the organization. A management job is a chancy affair, and therefore, seemingly not something that would be sought by a person with a strong need for job security.

Furthermore, if an individual in a management job performs in an unusual manner, be it either inferior or superior, he immediately becomes ''visible'' to those above him in the organization. To be inconspicuous is to be secure, for if one's actions are not out of the ordinary, one is not called to the attention of superiors and so no judgments are rendered. But being ''visible'' means that superiors are aware of one, and so performance outside of normal bounds is risky. Hence, the manager who performs exceptionally well cannot have a strong need for security.

On the basis of the foregoing arguments, we would have to say that the need for job security is not a part of managerial talent. Indeed, we would have to take just the opposite position, and posit the lack of job security to be a part of it.

The averages of the scores of the managers, supervisors, and workers on the scale measuring the strength of the need for job security are shown in Figure 9. It can be seen in the figure that the expected ordering of the three occupations in terms of average scores holds precisely, but that the direction is reversed so that managers tend to earn the lowest scores and workers the highest. Furthermore, the differences between the three groups are large.

The relationship between the scores that managers earn on the scale of need for job security and the degree of success they achieve in their executive and administrative positions is quite substantial. However, the relationship is in a negative direction so that it is those managers who have a strong need for job security who are less likely to be successful. That the relationship is negative is readily ascertained in Figure 10. The magnitude of the association is described by a coefficient of correlation of -0.30.

The ordering of the three occupational groups in terms of the degree of correlation between scores on the need for security scale and success can be seen in Figure 11. It is apparent that the necessary ordering holds, but that it, too, is in the reverse direction.

As is the case with the need for high financial reward, it is the lack of the need for job security which is a part of managerial talent. Those who seek entry into managerial jobs, and those who perform them best, tend to be people who have little need for job security. So the role of the need for security hypothesized earlier receives some verification.

COMPARATIVE CONTRIBUTION OF NEEDS
TO MANAGERIAL TALENT

As may be seen in Figures 9, 10, and 11, of the five needs here examined, only one apparently is unconnected with managerial talent, and that is the need for power over others. If this need has any bearing upon managerial talent, it is so slight as to be inconsequential. It would seem that those who have a strong drive to be managers and to perform their jobs well are not impelled by the desire for power over others and the authority connected with executive and administrative positions.

A second need, the need for high financial reward, does have some association with managerial talent, but that association is very slight. Furthermore, it is a negative one. That is, it is the lack of a need for high financial reward which plays a part in managerial talent. Those who seek managerial positions and achieve the greatest success in them are not likely to be driven by a desire for large amounts of pay.

A third need, the need for job security, seems to play a more important role than does the need for high financial reward, but like it, it does so in a negative fashion. It is the manager who has lesser rather than greater talent who is likely to have a strong need for security in his job. A willingness to accept a risk in connection with his job tends to be characteristic of the talented manager. Perhaps this is because he has faith in himself and belief in his abilities.

The last two needs, the need for occupational status and the need for self-actualization, both play a major role in managerial talent. Very likely, these two needs are not unrelated, for an individual who holds high position is more able to do what he wishes to, and to take the kinds of actions he believes are important and necessary. The fact that the need for high financial reward plays only a small part in managerial talent, and that the need for power over others has little or nothing to do with it, supports the position that the manager who seeks high position does not seek it especially for material or selfish ends; rather, it is a part of a more general desire to express himself, and to engage in creative activity.

6

SOME WARRANTED AND UNWARRANTED GENERALIZATIONS

W_e have finished our examination of the thirteen traits we chose for study. We have described the nature of each, and devised ways for measuring all of them. For better or for worse, we justified those methods of measurement. The part played by each trait in managerial talent has been studied. Now we wish to put all of the thirteen traits together in the same perspective in order to see which are of prime importance, and which play more modest roles or no roles at all. Identification of the relative importance of the various traits will permit us to ascertain something about the nature of managerial talent, and how it functions. In this chapter we shall also consider the careers of men of greater and lesser talent in one firm to illustrate how the utilization of managerial talent can help in the manpower planning of an organization. Finally, we shall examine the situation of the gifted manager in the organization. We shall want to ask such questions as, "How well does he fit into it?" and "Is the organization of such a character that his talents are fully utilized?"

THE RELATIVE IMPORTANCE OF THE VARIOUS TRAITS IN MANAGERIAL TALENT

We have individually studied our thirteen traits in some detail, seeing how each fits into the domain of managerial talent. We saw that the traits differ in their contribution to managerial talent, some contributing more and some less. We also saw that some of them did not even fall within the domain. In summary now, let us simultaneously compare all thirteen traits so that their relative contributions can be better assessed. This comparison will permit us to construct a picture of the nature of managerial talent.

Earlier we said that there are three conditions a trait must satisfy if it is to be considered a managerial trait. First, on the average managers should stand highest on the trait, line workers lowest, and line supervisors should fall between the two. If this is not the case and all three occupational groups have the same average, then the trait would not be more characteristic of managers than it is of those who are in other occupations. Supervisors should fall between managers and workers because they are quasi-management people. Second, there should be a substantial relationship for managers between the trait and their success. Should this not occur, then the trait could not be considered as being a part of managerial talent for it would be possessed to the same degree by good and poor executives and administrators. Finally, the relationship between the trait and job success should be highest for managers, lowest for workers, and at an intermediate degree for supervisors. If the relationship were the same for all three, it would mean that the trait is not a psychological property that is of unique importance for managerial performance. Rather, it would be a quality that is important in the performance of all manner of jobs. Again, since supervisors are quasi-managers they should be intermediate between the other two groups.

Obviously, a trait does not either completely satisfy these conditions, or completely fail to satisfy them. Rather, it satisfies them to various degrees. The ordering of the three occupational groups, whether in terms of averages or in terms of degrees of relationship between the trait and job success, might be perfect with the differences between the groups being large. Thus, the conditions with respect to averages or correlations with job success would be perfectly satisfied. In another instance, it might be that the managers and the supervisors are about the same and the line workers are different, or the supervisors and the line workers the same and the managers different. In such a case the condition can be considered to be fairly well satisfied. It is also possible for the managers to stand highest but for the supervisors and workers to be in reverse order from that which is expected. Then the condition would be even less well satisfied. Finally, all three occupational groups might be just about the same, or their order might bear no relationship whatsoever to the required one. In such a circumstance, it would have to be said that the condition is not satisfied at all. Similarly, the degree of relationship for managers between the trait and their success might be relatively high, moderate, or low, or there might even be no relationship at all. These gradations in the magnitude of the relationship indicate various degrees to which this particular condition is satisfied.

For each of the three conditions zero to five points representing the degree to which it was satisfied were assigned to every trait. The three values assigned a trait were added together in order to obtain a value which is a total or overall evaluation of it. While no trait satisfied all conditions to precisely the same degree, for all traits there was a good deal of agreement between its values for the three conditions. It will be understood that the assignment of these points was rather subjective and a matter of personal judgment. Nevertheless, the values do represent quantified descriptions of the extent to which the traits are important in managerial talent, and so permit us to describe the nature of that talent in more precise ways.

When the thirteen traits are assessed in this fashion, an ordering and positioning of them results, which is shown in Figure 12. First, it is quite obvious that supervisory ability has a unique position with respect to managerial talent. It is the trait which plays the most important role, and stands out clearly and is apart from all of the other traits. Following it is a cluster of five traits, the need for occupational achievement, intelligence, the need for self-actualization, self-assurance, and decisiveness. The traits in this cluster are just about equally important, and can be said to play a major role in managerial talent. Below them, and fairly well spread out, are the lack of the need for security and the lack of working class affinity, with initiative as a poor third. These three traits can be characterized as playing a minor role in managerial talent. There is a large gap between initiative and the remaining four traits. These last consist of the need for high financial reward, the need for power, maturity, and masculinity-femininity. Possibly the lack of the need for high financial reward might play a very small part in managerial talent, but quite obviously the other three traits do not fall within the domain of managerial talent, broad though it may be, and so have no pertinence to it whatsoever.

MANAGERIAL TALENT IN ONE FIRM: A CASE STUDY

We now have explored the domain of managerial talent, and have some notion of what it is like. We know that it includes supervisory ability, the need for occupational achievement, the need for self-actualization, intelligence, self-assurance, decisiveness, the lack of the need for security, the lack of working class affinity, and initiative, in that order of importance. We, of course, recognize that our exploration has by no means been exhaustive, and that there are many aspects of this complex human quality we have not even touched upon. Nevertheless, our examination has revealed some of the major characteristics of managerial talent so that we have a reasonable picture of it.

Now if the talent we have termed managerial talent is indeed that, and the nine traits listed above are components of it, we ought to be able to demonstrate in an independent circumstance that as a group those traits are related to success in management. Let us therefore perform a further experiment to provide the needed verification. For a separate group of managers, we shall combine the scores of the nine scales measuring the key traits, and relate them to other sorts of indices of success in management.

In our basic exploration we wanted to deal with as broad a group of managers as possible so that our findings would have a good deal of generality, thus, we drew a series of very small samples of managers from a wide variety of firms of different sorts. Furthermore, we examined the managers at only one period in their careers. For this experiment, let us instead take a fairly large number of managers in a single firm, and follow them over a long period of years. Furthermore, rather than using the judgments of supervisors as the index of success, let us use the actual administrative actions the firm has taken; that is, the negative action of termination of employment and the positive one of advancement to higher positions.

The firm selected for this experiment is a large financial organization with branch offices throughout most of the United States, as well as some overseas offices. The applicants for management positions in the firm were drawn from a variety of sources. About two-thirds came from other business establishments where generally they held either managerial or sales positions, and the other third were recent university graduates. Only a very few persons holding clerical or other lower positions in the firm itself were candidates for managerial positions in it, and, indeed, few appeared to be qualified for them. Candidates for managerial positions were evaluated entirely on the basis of interviews. An individual was first interviewed at the branch office to which he had applied, and then at the nearest regional headquarters. Each man was interviewed by four to eight different persons, and the decision of whether or not to hire was made at the regional headquarters, where the evaluations made by the various interviewers were collated.

This particular firm was selected because it carefully follows the performance of its managers, keeps good records of their activities, and periodically reviews each individual. As a consequence, the administrative actions it took with respect to its managers in the form of termination of employment and advancement in position were based almost entirely upon performance rather than upon seniority, education, previous experience, and other similar factors.

During a three-year period the Self-Description Inventory, the basic test used in our exploration of managerial talent, was administered to a large proportion of candidates for the firm's managerial jobs. Although it was administered as if it were a regular part of the assessment procedures, the scores on it were in fact not used in the evaluation of the candidates. The careers of eighty-one men who were hired during this three-year period were followed in the firm for as long as twenty years.

As a measure of initial success in management, those new men who were retained by the firm for three years or more were considered to be successful, and those who were retained for less than three years, or who resigned within their first three years of employment, were classified as being failures. Ten to 15 years after they were hired, the survivors were considered for advancement to high positions in the firm, and some of them were actually advanced. Before this, of course, there had been advancements to intermediate levels. These high positions were just below the vice-presidential level, and so were jobs of considerable substance.

It is to be noted that at the time of this experiment all of those men who were advanced to the high positions had held them for at least two years, and all were considered by the firm to be successful in them. Indeed, none had been released or transferred, or voluntarily left the firm. Of the original group of eighty-one managers, 26 percent failed within the first three years, and 12 percent were advanced to the high positions 10 to 18 years later.

On the basis of the total scores they earned on the scales measuring the nine key traits listed earlier, the eighty-one men were divided into four levels of managerial talent: those with high total scores, those with high average scores, those with low average scores, and those with low scores. The total score indicating degree of managerial talent was obtained simply by adding together for each individual his scores on the scales measuring the nine key traits. The scores on the scales for the need for security and working class affinity were reversed so that a high score indicates a low amount of the trait and a low score a high amount. This was effected by subtracting an individual's score from the highest possible score on the scale. By this procedure the scores on these two scales measured a lack of the two traits.

The chart in Figure 13 shows the outcomes in terms of success in management for the man in each of the four levels of managerial talent. Of the men who earned high total scores, 90 percent succeeded in lower managerial positions, and a quarter of them were advanced to, and succeeded in, the upper echelons of the firm. Only 10 percent of these men were unable to master the executive and administrative activities at the lowest managerial levels, and could be considered failures. At the other extreme, two-thirds of the men who made low total scores failed even at the very lowest levels of management, and none of them attained higher positions in the firm. As may be seen in Figure 13, the men who earned scores intermediate between the highest and lowest levels of managerial talent achieved intermediate degrees of success in management.

This experiment, then, provides the independent verification needed to show that as a group the traits of supervisory ability, the need for occupational achievement, the need for self-actualization, intelligence, self-assurance, decisiveness, the lack of the need for security, the lack of working class affinity, and initiative, do in fact describe managerial talent. In this experimental firm, the greater the individual's managerial talent, the more likely he was to succeed as a manager at the lower levels, and the higher was the probability that he ultimately would reach the highest levels of management. If the firm had employed only those men who possessed the highest level of managerial talent as measured by total scores on the nine scales, it would have been far better off. The initial loss in managers would have been reduced by more than 60 percent, and the number of managers capable of operating at the highest echelons of the firm would have been more than doubled.

THE FABRIC OF MANAGERIAL TALENT

Our explorations of managerial talent have shown that of all of the qualities which form its fabric, it is the capacity to direct and to guide the efforts and actions of others which is the dominant element. Leadership, then, colors the entire plaid of the material which is managerial talent. It is the prime feature which characterizes and distinguishes it. To many this will not seem surprising, for they emphasize the manager's role as a supervisor. But as we have pointed out, supervision is only one of the manager's many duties, and often, if not ordinarily, the number of people he directly supervises is quite small. Even so, it is true that by holding a position above the lowest level of the organizational hierarchy, the manager is at least indirectly responsible for the activities of a large number of persons. As a consequence, the talented manager, the one whose performance is outstanding, must necessarily have as one of his primary concerns the behavior and welfare of the many who hold positions below him in the organization.

The traits of intelligence, self-assurance, decisiveness, and the needs for occupational achievement and self-actualization form a cluster of qualities which are somewhat less important for managerial talent than is supervisory ability. It is apparent that the talented manager seeks position in the organization, and at the same time wishes to utilize his talents to the fullest and to utilize them in work which is of significance. He wants both high occupational status and the opportunity for self-actualization. The fact that the successful manager is endowed with the qualities represented in intellectual superiority means that he is fully capable of doing that work. By this high level of intellect he is further distinguished from his less successful colleague. His machinery is geared to climb the steep road ahead. The talented manager is further equipped for his task by the very fact that he believes he is well endowed, and is prepared to utilize his abilities. He is both self-assured and decisive.

We are left with the three traits of lack of a need for security, lack of working class affinity, and initiative as being parts of managerial talent, though parts which are lesser in importance than the ones we have just discussed. These three traits seem to have little or nothing in common, and to pertain to quite different aspects of human qualities. Our exploration indicates that the need for security carries no weight at all for the talented executive and administrator. Indeed, quite the contrary, security even appears to be something he avoids. He is a person who is willing to take risks, rather than one who seeks self-protective circumstances. Furthermore, the talented manager is not one who has a "we-feeling" with working class people. In fact, he tends to be the sort of person blue-collar workers would reject as a co-worker. Finally, to some extent the talented manager is one who can readily initiate necessary action, and at the same time can see new and different solutions to problems.

Having, as it were, obtained a notion of the nature of the warp and the woof of the fabric that is managerial talent, let us now try to see what general pattern is formed by the interweaving of the threads. We have seen what the details are, so let us now generalize—and even over-generalize—so as to obtain a picture of managerial talent in its very broadest perspective. It is possible to discern four major features of the pattern of managerial talent, features which form an integrated and meaningful whole. The four features are an aloof democratic leadership, a creative and effective intelligence, a faith in oneself, and the desire for achievement.

We have seen that leadership is a most important element in the managerial job. Inasmuch as there are a whole host of different ways in which the superior can act in order to influence the behavior and thinking of his subordinates, a wide variety of leadership styles is clearly possible. On the basis of the findings with our managers, it might be said that a major feature of managerial talent is what might be termed a restrained democratic type of leadership.

The evidence obtained in our exploration indicates that the strength of the need for power over others is completely unrelated to success in executive and administrative positions. The effective managers were found to have no greater or lesser desire for power than the ineffective ones. As a consequence, it would seem to follow that when our good managers were exercising leadership they were not doing it in a unilateral, command fashion. Rather, it seems likely that they would utilize the alternative—democratic leadership, that kind of supervision wherein the superior invites his subordinates to participate in the government of the work group.

In addition, it was seen that the talented manager manifests a lack of working class affinity. That is, he is not the sort of person who is accepted as one of their own by those who labor, and he in turn does not identify with them. Indeed, working class people would set him apart from themselves, and he in turn would differentiate himself from them. There is, then, a social separation between the superior manager and those who work for him, at least those at the lower levels of the organization. In other words, the manager is aloof from those whose activities he supervises; he is restrained in his relationships with them. He would not be a buddy-buddy, or a father confessor kind of boss. On the contrary, it must be the case that his relationships with his subordinates are formal, formal in the sense that they are concerned principally, if not entirely, with the problems connected with the organization's activities, and not with problems pertaining to personal matters. This situation would permit the manager to have an impartiality in dealing with his subordinates, and they in turn would not be saddled with a boss who insists in sticking his nose into their private affairs. The relationships between the superior manager and those he supervises might well be characterized as being businesslike. It perhaps is not unlike the traditional, and certainly idealized, relationship between a ship's captain and his crew. The skipper, of course, is solely and entirely responsible fot the ship's mission. In addition, he is responsible for the welfare of the men; nonetheless, he is apart from them not only socially but physically as well. Thus, he is presumed to be in an impartial position with respect to his men so that they are judged without bias, and are dealt with fairly in their work.

The second feature of the pattern of managerial talent pertains to intelligence. The minds of different sorts of individuals operate in different ways. The intellect of some gives the impression of sheer power. Problems are met head on, and are dealt with by a massive analysis and logic. The intellect of others seems more rapier-like. These individuals probe a problem with a series of sharp jabs, each of which deals with a portion of the matter quickly but perhaps without providing total solutions. From the evidence at hand, the mentality of superior managers would seem to be best described as a kind of creative and effective intelligence.

Intelligence is one of the traits which was found in this investigation, as well as other investigations, to be an important determiner of success in executive and managerial jobs. The successful manager is a very bright person. He can analyze and reason. His judgment is excellent. His capacity to understand and to learn are exceptional. Because of his superior powers of ideational synthesis, he is far better than most in formulating plans.

In addition to intelligence, we found that decisiveness and the need for self-actualization also are important strands of the web of managerial talent. We saw that initiative, too, is involved, although to a somewhat lesser extent. Since these other qualities fall within the domain of managerial talent, they give a particular slant, a further meaning, to the nature of the intelligence of gifted managers.

The fact that the superior manager is decisive suggests that when he is confronted with a problem, he immediately directs his full powers of analysis and reasoning in sharp focus upon it. Support for this notion is provided by his strength in initiative, for this means that he has the capacity to respond quickly and to act readily. Very likely, he is not one who is given to an easy-going and reflective consideration of a matter in its broad and theoretical setting purely as a mental exercise. Rather, his attention would be totally and completely turned to the heart of the issue, seeking quick and practical solutions. His intelligence, then, is of a highly practical sort.

Those who have a strong need for self-actualization have no interest whatsoever in trivialities. Their concern is with the utilization of their abilities in dealing with problems which are of substantial significance, problems that have a complication and depth, and problems which need original approaches and not just a choice among obvious alternatives. The thinking of those who have a high degree of initiative is not tightly channeled. Rather, it is characterized by fluidity and flexibility. Such people are able to rearrange their bits and pieces of knowledge in meaningful ways that others may well overlook, and they have novel insights about possible solutions to problems. They are original thinkers. Inasmuch as superior managers stand high both in the need for self-actualization and in initiative, their kind of intellect would appear to be creative.

The mental aspects of managerial talent can therefore be termed a creative and effective intelligence. It is an intelligence which is forceful and sharp, while at the same time it is insightful and innovative.

A third feature of the pattern of managerial talent is highlighted by a group of traits, all of which bear upon self-confidence. These traits center around self-assurance, and include self-actualization, decisiveness, and the lack of a need for security.

We demonstrated that self-assurance is a true managerial trait inasmuch as it related to performance in executive and administrative positions, and differentiates people holding such positions from those in lower positions in the organization. The outstanding manager has a high degree of confidence in himself. He is certain that he possesses abilities fully commensurate with the problems he is called upon to handle, and as a consequence believes he can handle them in an effective manner. There is no question in his mind about his competence.

The talented manager's strong need for self-actualization is further evidence of his belief in his capacities. For people in whom this need is strong necessarily start out with the presumption that they have outstanding qualities, otherwise they would not seek important and significant tasks.

The fact that the superior manager stands high in decisiveness and low in the need for security is testimony to his confidence in himself. The decisive person has no compunctions about taking action. He is perfectly willing to go ahead and do what needs to be done. In part this is likely because he considers the action to be a good and a justifiable one. But his lack of a need for security must mean that he does not require support from others or from the circumstances of work; rather, he is assured that he has whatever qualities are required to tackle the task successfully. It is on these grounds that he proceeds to action.

From the foregoing it is apparent that faith in one's self is a third feature of managerial talent. This faith gives the individual the inner strength to go ahead on his own, and while it does not mean he is unconcerned about outcomes and never questions himself, it does indicate that the talented manager is fully able to withstand, and even to ignore, the threat of failure. Indeed, quite the contrary, the faith in one's self frees the person of undue worry about his security and safety so that he can go ahead and act in truly constructive and creative ways.

The fourth and final feature which characterizes and distinguishes the overall pattern of managerial talent is the need for achievement. We have seen that those managers who are exceptionally good at their jobs have strong positive motivations. They stand high, and just about equally so, in the need for occupational achievement and in the need for self-actualization.

The need on the part of superior managers for occupational achievement, a desire to attain high positions in their business or industrial establishments, must be considered to be a positive type of striving. Certainly, these managers do not seek such positions for the high financial remuneration that goes with them, since the desire for high pay was shown to be completely outside the domain of managerial talent. Therefore, the striving upward in the organization is not for personal gain. Nor is it a reflection of some consuming wish to control the behavior and thinking of others, to dictate what subordinates will and will not do. This is evidenced by the fact that the need for power is no more characteristic of successful managers than it is for others in the organization. Furthermore, the upward striving cannot be ascribed as a desire for security. It could be that seeking high position in an organization is really a way of attaining security, for high position is walled in by great authority and high status; thus it provides a considerable measure of protection. However, we have also seen that superior managers do not desire security, and, indeed, security is something that they actually eschew.

Consequently, it would appear that the upward striving on the part of managers who manifest excellence in their work is not the result of ambition for personal gain, or for other similar sorts of private ends. The fact that they have a very strong need for self-actualization involves utilizing one's talents fully, so that the individual's personality is given full and creative expression. It also involves the direction of one's efforts to tasks that are of significance, and society is the judge of the significance of a task. In effect, superior managers' need for achievement is founded on a desire for challenges, challenges of an intellectual sort, challenges which pertain to the solution of problems that are of social consequence. The need for achievement permits the superior manager to mobilize his efforts, and directs them to matters which are meaningful.

From the foregoing arguments we are led to the conclusion that the general properties of managerial talent are a restrained democratic leadership, a creative and effective intelligence, a faith in one's self, and a desire for achievement. The successful manager utilizes democratic procedures when dealing with his subordinates, but at the same time keeps himself apart from them so as to maintain an impartial position. He is a very bright person, and his intellect is forceful, practical, and constructive. He recognizes that he possesses these qualities, and so he has the confidence that is so necessary if he is to successfully deal with complex executive and administrative problems. Finally, he is a highly motivated person, one who is fully capable of maintaining his goal of orientation, his goals being quite worthwhile ones.

The picture we have put together of the individual with high managerial talent may seem to be a paragon of all of the virtues. But this is not really the case. We see nothing special in him of the compassion of the physician, the concentration of the scientist, the dedication of the jurist, or the reflective contemplation of the philosopher. We are therefore not describing that rare individual who could equally well be senator, prelate, general, or corporation president. Those persons who have high managerial talent might well be ill-fitted for occupations other than the executive and administrative. Admittedly, managerial talent is a broad quality, but by no means do those who possess it to a high degree automatically qualify for any and all exalted positions in our society. Nevertheless, the individual who has high managerial talent is a very special person, one who has quite desirable qualities, and one who can make a real contribution to his organization and to society.

CASE HISTORIES OF SOME TALENTED
AND UNTALENTED MANAGERS

We have been mainly talking from statistics, and even though they are statistics about people they are but cold facts which do not convey the feeling of the human drama. Let us now look at some individual managers, managers who differ in their talent for executive and administrative jobs. Two of these managers are superior in talent, and two of them inferior. It was on the grounds of their scores on the research test of managerial traits that they were classified as being talented or untalented. The two superior managers earned generally high scores on the scales of supervisory ability, intelligence, the need for self-actualization, self-assurance, decisiveness, and initiative, and low scores on the need for security, and working class affinity. The two inferior managers had just the opposite pattern of scores on these scales. As was the case with all of the managers in the study, these four took the test in connection with an assessment for some personnel action such as advancement to a higher level position in the same organization, or selection for a job in a different firm. All four men were between twenty-five and thirty-five years of age when they took the test. However, the following descriptions of their careers cover periods both before and after the time of testing.

The careers of these four men are typical of those of talented and untalented managers. Nevertheless, it must be admitted that the individuals were chosen systematically rather than randomly. In part, they were selected to represent different sorts of business and industrial careers. Certainly, consciously or unconsciously, they were also chosen so as to provide a tidy picture of the relationship between managerial talent and managerial success. Nevertheless, two of the men are both talented and successful, and two of them both untalented and unsuccessful, and it is in this sense that they are illustrative.

The first of our successful managers served a tour of duty in the Army after graduating from college, and so perhaps was a bit more mature than most men entering the job market for the first time. Because he believed opportunities were better in a small company than in a large one, he took a position as a salesman with a family-owned firm that manufactured precision instruments of a highly specialized sort. Even though he had no technical background he developed a thorough understanding of the firm's products through diligent study, and became a very productive salesman. Because of his aggressiveness in sales he was made sales manager. In this position he induced the company to apply their instrumentation and expertise to the development and production of new products. The broadened line proved to be a moneymaker, and he was rewarded by being appointed general manager. After enjoying further success in this position by reorganizing and improving operations, he was made a partner, and ultimately president. When he joined the firm it had been experiencing lean times, and largely as a result of his efforts both in the promotion and development of its products, and in the improvement of operating procedures in the plant, it became strong. Indeed, the firm's position was so good that a larger competitive company made such a handsome offer that the partners could not refuse it. Now financially independent at the age of forty-five, he was at loose ends. Although he could have retired and lived most comfortably, he could not bring himself to accept a life of inactivity. He therefore became a member of a firm which purchased and reconstructed small unsuccessful businesses. Again his efforts were so very successful that here, too, he soon ended up in top management. Clearly, this is a career that must be described as thoroughly successful, the success being the entire result of the man's talents, and not of fortuitous circumstances.

The second of our talented men was born to wealth. He attended an "ivy league" college where, incidentally, he made Phi Beta Kappa. Since he was in the ROTC program, upon graduation he was called to duty in the Army. He was sent to England to be a trouble-shooter in a liaison position between two parallel British and American military units. These two units were getting along very poorly, and largely because of his tact and social sensitivity he soon eased relationships between the two antagonistic groups. This won him an early promotion. Nevertheless, when he was eligible for release from the Army after two years, he left it in order to enter graduate school where in three years he earned his doctorate degree in economics. He then joined a firm which dealt with quite large real estate projects, both industrial and otherwise. His task was one of analysis and evaluation of property, and of prospects for its utilization and sale. He proved most adept at this, and so moved up in the firm. However, he found the action too slow, and the firm's policies too conservative for his taste, and he decided to seek a more challenging career. Now in his early thirties, he went with a financial organization which was alert, progressive, and moving. Here he began in a position at the lowest level of management. Again, his competence manifested itself, and in a few years he was made second in charge in a regional office, being advanced over the heads of a number of older men. He was in effect being "stored," for the firm regarded him as being top quality material, and his immediate superior was scheduled for retirement in a few years. He became the regional manager, and ran his division so well and so profitably that by the time he was 40 he was made a member of the governing body of the firm. Again, we have a clear case of a man who performed exceedingly well as a manager. Inasmuch as he had private means, quite obviously his way up was not the financial struggle that it is for most young men. In this way, then, his path was eased, and he could afford to take risks in changing organizations. However, it is pertinent to note that this man is a member of a racial minority, and therefore had a clear handicap. Nevertheless, so great was his talent that he operated with a high degree of effectiveness in quite diverse circumstances.

The first of our less talented men came from a "good" family. He attended a "good" college where he achieved some distinction socially and in athletics, but none in scholastic endeavors. Through his family connections, and not as a result of his own efforts, he obtained a position in the bookkeeping department of an investment brokerage firm. He had wanted to be a stock and bond salesman, but both he and the company realized he just did not have the aggressiveness and the mental sharpness that was necessary. After eight years he became head of the accounting department, and by the time he reached his fortieth year he was made supervisor of the firm's clerical operations. The firm had made it clear to him that he could expect no further advancements, for while his work was adequate, it was only minimally so. Furthermore, they considered his ability insufficient to handle higher level assignments. So at the age of forty-seven he left the firm, and with some increase in income he joined a small local real estate agency where he dealt principally in the rental of residential properties and apartments. The picture of this man's career as a manager is quite unimpressive, showing a slow rate of advancement and a final plateau at a low managerial level. While the firm considered that his work left much to be desired, they did not deem it sufficiently poor to release him. Anyway, they thought that they had probably made a mistake in raising him to the position of office supervisor, and so felt somewhat responsible for him. Then, too, there was his "good" family with whom the top management of the company was acquainted. So the continuity of his employment with the firm and such advances as he received were not really a function of his personal qualities, but rather most kindly can be ascribed to "circumstances."

The second untalented man entered college knowing that he wanted to be an accountant and he achieved very high grades in that subject. Upon graduation, he had no difficulty in joining an excellent and respected firm of certified public accountants where soon his occupational interest was matched by the proficiency he attained in his work. As a consequence, he was given more and more complex and difficult accounts to handle. After some six years he was "stolen" by a company that was one of the accounting firm's clients whom he had been serving, the company being much impressed with his thoroughness and knowledge. He was made head of the accounting division, and did a good job of tidying it up, which it well needed. The heads of other divisions in the company did not regard him too favorably, complaining that he insisted on "sticking to the book," was not cooperative, and was very slow in providing needed information and services. Nevertheless, he was raised to the position of comptroller because the top management of the company continued to be impressed with the tightness of his accounting systems. In this new position he was called upon to take a broad view of company matters, to work closely with others, and above all, to make quick decisions of far-ranging consequence. He did not like the duties connected with the position of comptroller, the responsibilities were weightier than he wanted to carry, and after a few years he just up and quit. Still thinking of himself as a high level manager he took a position that was labeled "treasurer" in a small company that was dying, and he knew full well had no future. Indeed, his task was to take care of the financial matters in its dissolution. In a couple of years the company did fold its tent, and there he was after 20 years back where he began, seeking employment as an accountant. Here is a career with initial growth and promise followed by a later decline, a career that is sad for it left the man at middle age with a life that was singularly unfilled. Although by no means an ungifted person, his capabilities just did not include managerial talent. Clearly, this man should have stayed in the technical area where he was indeed singularly competent, and should not have attempted a career in management.

These four cases illustrate some of the major differences between the careers of talented managers and their less gifted colleagues. Those managers who possess high levels of managerial talent do their work well and advance rapidly up the organizational ladder. When their occupational lives are completed they have reached high executive and administrative positions. If they change from one firm to another it is likely to be because their job with the first is not fulfilling, and the second promises more personal satisfaction and allied rewards. Those men of lesser managerial talent perform their jobs in quite a pedestrian manner, and achieve little by way of advancement in status. At their retirement they terminate their careers at rather low levels in the organizational hierarchy. When they leave a firm it is likely to be for a nonmanagerial job, for they find themselves to be unsuited for executive and administrative duties and responsibilities.

THE GIFTED MANAGER AND THE ORGANIZATION

If one wants music and says that a pianist rather than a flautist, a violinist, or a trumpeter should play, then quite obviously one is specifying that it is piano music which is desired, and not flute, violin, or trumpet music. In fact, by stipulating the particular type of talent the musician should have, one is thereby designating for the given situation the particular kind of music that is to be considered good music. So if one hires a pianist, and expects him to play flute, violin, or trumpet music, and then complains when he plays piano music, obviously one is out of one's mind, or at the very least, confused.

Furthermore, if one says that one wants piano music, and that therefore a pianist should do the playing rather than a flautist, a violinist, or a trumpeter, one must provide him with a piano. A flute, a violin, or a trumpet just will not do, for the musician's special talent does not lie in playing them, but in playing the piano. It would be absolutely ridiculous to hire a pianist and provide him with a flute, a violin, or a trumpet, but not with a piano, and then complain because he does not play piano music.

Similarly, if an organization says that it wants as executives and administrators men who stand high in those qualities we have described here as constituting managerial talent, rather than men with other sorts of talents, then it is saying that it wants its affairs managed by men who exercise a restrained democratic leadership and who possess an effective and creative intelligence, a faith in one's self, and a desire for achievement. In fact, by stipulating that these are the sorts of managers it wants, the organization is thereby designating what it considers to be good management. If it hires men high in these qualities, expecting them to manage its affairs in ways not commensurate with their talents, and then complains because they do not, obviously that organization is out of its mind, or at the very least, confused.

Furthermore, if the organization does say that indeed this is the kind of management it wants, and so chooses as executives and administrators men with the qualities we have termed managerial talent, then it must provide them with the circumstances whereby they can fulfill their restrained democratic leadership, effective and creative intelligence, faith in themselves, and desire for achievement. Other circumstances just will not do, for under them the men's special talents could not possibly manifest themselves. It would be absolutely ridiculous for the organization to hire men with these qualities, and then complain because those qualities are not exercised in the management of its affairs.

Therefore, it is pertinent to inquire into the kinds of circumstances in business and industrial establishments which do not provide support for talented managers. We are interested in the characteristics of the managerial job, and of conditions within the organization, which preclude talented managers from exercising the particular sorts of qualities they possess. Obviously, all firms are not the same, and even those that are competitors in precisely the same field face different problems, have different needs, and seek different objectives. More importantly, they have different histories, and in the course of their development have evolved different traditions and modes of operation.

It is apparent, then, that there are innumerable circumstances within business and industrial firms that can preclude the effectualization of the qualities of talented managers. Furthermore, since firms differ so much among themselves it seems obvious that there is a good deal of specificity of these circumstances in different individual firms, some of them occurring in certain firms and others in different ones. But at least, we ought to be able to list some of the kinds of circumstances which foster the characteristics we evolved as being the four general features of managerial talent. Let us examine these features and see if we can deduce some of the kinds of circumstances which inhibit their manifestation.

The first major feature of managerial talent that we discerned is a restrained democratic leadership. So if a firm fails to give their managers positions wherein they can direct and guide the efforts of others, and be responsible for their actions, the firm will not be making full use of their talented men. Furthermore, they cannot be expected to be autocratic in their relationships with their subordinates, but at the same time they must be permitted to maintain some social distance from them.

We have seen that in a substantial number of executive and administrative positions the individual supervises few people, and in many his supervision is indirect. This is the very nature of the case in business and industrial organizations, and must be accepted as such. Nevertheless, we also saw that during his career the manager moves from position to position, and these positions differ in their duties. Hence, at least occasionally he can be placed in jobs wherein he does directly supervise others. In any event, it would appear that to maintain a man perpetually in purely staff positions would be undesirable. If nothing else, the firm, through its training or management development programs ought to make the individual aware that his position in the managerial hierarchy makes him in fact responsible for many people at levels below his, distant though they may appear to him.

Following are some typical remarks about this matter made by managers themselves:

> It's great being in jobs like this where I am making policy that affects the whole operation. I'm a big shot, and I like it. But I don't want to stay here forever. Sometime I want to get out on the firing line, seeing that the fellows in the shop get the nuts on the bolts.

> I think it is only because I had time as a first-line supervisor, and then put in a few years in second- and third-line supervision that I have a feel for how this whole operation works. I'm doing this management job a whale of a lot better than those lads who never even called a roll in the morning.

> I almost have the feeling that the plans and recommendations I work out and send on go right to the machines in the plant, untouched by human hands, and unseen by human eyes. It's an impersonal operation, and I don't feel I have any control over what is happening below.

The talented manager has no particular taste for power. Whatever drive he may have for power over others does not set him apart from his less gifted colleagues. In any event, his leadership would not be authoritarian, and this would leave democratic procedures as the alternative for him. Consider some characteristic statements concerning power made by managers.

> The big boss says you have to lay down the law to get people to do anything. But that's silly, and I told him so. These people are grown-up men, and they wouldn't take that sort of stuff even if there wasn't a union. These are skilled men, and they know what they are doing.
>
> No, I don't have regular meetings with my department heads, but we do all get together every three or four weeks or so, when it seems necessary to work out things for the whole division. But I spend a lot of time with them individually, or maybe with two or three of them together. After all, between them they have an awful lot of experience, and I sure want to take advantage of that. Anyway, each one knows his part of the operation a lot better than I do, and I damn well better listen to what they have to say.
>
> These men and women who are working for me are human beings, and should be treated as such. They deserve to have their say, and they deserve to be told about what is going on. I know I expect my boss to treat me that way.

The talented manager believes that there ought to be some social distance between him and those he supervises. It appears necessary to him that the superior should remain at least somewhat aloof from those whose actions he directs. If the organization permits this, he works well; if it does not, then he may be unhappy. Here are some representative views of managers.

> I got good and sore at those people from personnel. This guy comes over and tells me I have to have some private sessions with each of my men to tell them how they are doing, and to help them with any problems they might have here or at home which affect their work. I told him I have always made a point of telling each man in my department exactly where he stands with me, but that I am no handholding shrinker man, and the private lives of these people are none of my business, or his business, or the business of anyone in the company.
>
> Occasionally I have lunch with one of the men who works for me, but only when we have something about our operation to discuss and time is a problem. Otherwise I do not socialize with

my section chiefs. As a department head, I have to judge them, and it is impossible to judge your friends impartially, yet this is what I am paid to do.

Some of the other supervisors have a yearly department picnic where both the foremen and the line workers go. But I don't, because a picnic is a time to have fun, and who can let themselves go in front of the boss. Anyway, I can't see drinking beer and eating hot dogs with a man one day, and disciplining him the next.

We found that an effective and creative intelligence is a second major feature of managerial talent. Any circumstances existing in the firm which do not make use of the talented manager's nimble mind with its decisiveness and originality is failing to realize the potential which exists in its executives and administrators. Perhaps the one circumstance which more than any other defeats the talented manager is a rigid bureaucracy. In part, this is a result of a fear of failure, or rather the fear of the reprisals which come from failure, on the part of those in positions of responsibility. A policy which heavily weights the protection of infinite caution over action kills the talented manager. Oftentimes a rigid bureaucracy is sheerly the result of the aging of the organization, a hardening of its arteries. The firm has become so immutable that however well worked out and justifiable a proposal may be, if it is at all at variance with established policies and procedures it will not be accepted, for these policies and procedures are unchangeable. The talented manager could probably tolerate outright rejection of his proposals, since that is a definite action, but in a rigid bureaucracy his proposals simply get lost in the great, intricate, and amorphous network of the firm's administrative offices, never again to see the light of day. As much as it stifles decisiveness, so much more does a rigid bureaucracy dampen creativity. For creativity is uniqueness, and this is something that bureaucracy cannot tolerate.

The talented manager has the capacity to solve problems in ways which are useful and practical. That is, he will grant the traditions and modes of operation that exist in the firm, providing, of course, that they are not of the rigid bureaucratic sort. He may not entirely like them, but the solutions to problems he develops will be possible of execution within the particular given framework. Furthermore, he is forceful in the way in which he solves problems. He utilizes whatever information he can command, integrating it in the most meaningful fashion, and then readily acts upon it when action is necessary. Certainly, any firm would approve of a manager who works out practical solutions to problems. But too often the firm requires him to develop solutions which have to meet absurd requirements, and have to be cleared with people who have at best only a remote concern with, or knowledge of, the problem. In many instances the firm will not support the man who is willing to stick his neck out, and pushing courses of action because he is convinced that action is necessary. The firm too often frowns upon the individual who makes waves. Managers express themselves on this matter in the following ways:

> No one knows everything about a problem, and no one ever can. The point is that you have to do what has to be done, and you usually have to do it within a pretty short time limit. You do the very best you can to get as much of the data as is possible, and you try to put together a picture. But it is never perfect, and mostly it is pretty far from it. You use your head to work out as good a solution as is possible under the circumstances. However, imperfect as it may be you have to use it and go ahead and act, because if you don't the whole operation will slow down.

> You have to figure out practical answers. By practical, I mean plans that are workable, and can be executed within the policies and facilities of the company. You've got to be sure that your plan will do the job, stay within the budget, and will not put too much pressure on the rest of the crowd. Otherwise, it is just theory and theory which is pretty remote from reality.

> One of the reasons I left that company is because paperwork is sacred there, and getting the job done is only of minor importance. Everything has to be cleared with everybody, and in this competitive market you just can't afford to wait. I would sweat blood and sit up nights developing a plan that would really work, and it would just seem to disappear. If I looked around enough, I'd probably find it sitting in somebody's in-basket, or more likely in his hold-basket, because he just hadn't gotten around to review it. I spent a lot of time learning about the productive and marketing capacities of this company, and I know pretty well what

they can and can't do. Anyway, even though they complained because I went out of channels, I always checked every plan I made with the production and marketing people before I submitted it. So I knew my plans were OK. But to do things the way the company wants them done takes just too much effort, and the result is just not constructive.

In addition to being effective, the mind of the talented manager also has the quality of being creative. That is, the talented manager is an originator, an innovator, one who can work out novel solutions to problems. A rigid bureaucracy, as we have seen, stifles this quality. Even where bureaucracy is not a factor, there often is a tendency to hesitate in accepting possible courses of action that are different, just because they are different. This seems incomprehensible to the talented manager, for otherwise the firm may be alert, progressive, and always ready for action. It must be recognized, of course, that all jobs in an organization do not require creativity. There always are some routine operations which must be accomplished. Insofar as possible, talented managers should not be assigned to them, or should be assigned to them for as short periods as feasible. But even so, there are relatively few managerial jobs where some creativity is not possible. Consequently, the firm can afford to foster innovation whatever the individual's assignment in it may be.

Managers' concern with innovation and creativity can be seen in the following examples.

> When I first came into this department the boss told me what they needed most of all was new ideas. He said that whenever I have what looks like a good idea not to let loose of it, and to give it all I have. He told me not to worry about the job, and that he'll cover for me if it is absolutely necessary that I miss some time. Especially he stressed my accounting background, and said that even though I might not now see any application to this kind of operation, and he certainly didn't, I was to keep thinking about it, and not to worry about ideas which don't pan out. What a boss. But I guess he'll never make VP.
>
> I hate to brag, but I do have my division running smoothly—so smoothly in fact that they hardly even need me in emergencies.

I want it this way because this gives me a lot of time just to sit and think, and especially to think about improvements. Because no matter how well my division is running, I know that there are always better ways of doing things, and I aim to find them. I am always frightened that we will become static, and freeze our administration so that we won't be able to keep moving ahead. Conditions are always changing, and we have to change to meet them.

The third feature of managerial talent is faith in one's self. Faith in one's self means that the individual is confident of his ability to do those executive and administrative assignments he seeks, and is willing to accept the full responsibility for doing them. If it is to make optimal use of its talented managers, the firm should take advantage of the fact that the talented manager has confidence in himself by placing him in positions where his activities do have a significant impact upon the operation, and where he must take decisive and definitive action. This means, of course, that the firm must be careful to distinguish between the capable manager who justifiably is confident, and the less able man who is simply conceited. The remarks below are illustrative of how managers regard self-confidence.

In this business, you are dealing completely with intangibles. You never really know whether what you are doing is right or wrong. Or at least any feedback you get comes so late it is of no real help. So you have to believe in your self; you have to believe that you have analyzed the situation well, and that your judgment is good. You just go ahead and do the deed, and then forget about it. If you have confidence in your own ability, you can cut it; otherwise you ought to be in a different game.

I have no compunctions at all in taking on the responsibility of heading up this plant. Maybe I am a little young, but I have the training and experience both in production and in management that is necessary, so I think I am quite capable of running the show. I have spent time in different plants and branch offices of this firm, and some in the central office, so I have been tested and proved in a lot of different phases of the company's operation. I don't think I'm any genius, and I make my share of mistakes. I know I have limitations. But I also know that I have assets, and I think my assets far outweigh my limitations. If I didn't, I wouldn't have come into this business in the first place.

When things break we have to move fast, and so I have to phone my field representatives right away and tell them what action to take. This means I can't give them anywhere near the full background for the move. So they have to go ahead pretty much in the dark, and trust that I know what I'm doing. Well, if I'm not convinced that I'm taking the right steps, I can't see how these people could have any confidence in me, or in what I'm telling them to do. I've been a field representative, and I know what it's like. If the fellow in the home office is at all uncertain about the action, you can't charge out all fired up and do a definitive job. That's why I take as much care as I can in working up plans in the short time I have, so that I am sure of them.

I left that firm because I wanted to transfer to a job in operations, and they wouldn't give me one. They had me doing staff functions, and there was no prospect of me getting out of them even in the distant future. When I first went with the firm, I had a job as assistant supervisor and did well at it. Well enough to earn an early promotion. So I have good grounds for thinking I have what it takes, and I want responsibility and action. Being in planning has been an interesting experience, and I'm glad I had it. I learned a lot about this firm and about this industry. But I didn't want to spend the rest of my life working up data and making recommendations for somebody else to use.

The fourth and final general feature of managerial talent is the need for achievement. The talented manager wants to be sure that what he is doing is of significance. In some cases this is obvious, but if it is not, then it is up to the firm to convince the individual in one way or another that his efforts are directed to matters which are of consequence, and are not just part of a crass endeavor whose sole object is to make profits. Management training and development should be as much concerned with the social "why" of the firm, as with the "how" of its operation. Unless the talented manager can see his activities as being a real part of the big scheme, even though his own particular contribution be small, he will not have the sense of achievement that he wants and needs. Power, status, and money are important to him, but not primarily for themselves alone. Isolated they do not properly motivate him; for him they are means to a larger goal of achievement in meaningful activities. Here are some pertinent statements made by managers on this topic.

The thing I like about this business is that it is really the whole foundation of all business. That's why I chose finance to begin with, and that's why I stay in it. I know that what I am doing is important. There are other kinds of businesses where I could work and be quite happy, and probably make a lot more money. But I just don't think that any of them would give me quite the degree of satisfaction that finance does, and my salary is quite satisfactory. All business is important, but to my way of thinking, finance is really the keystone.

Sure I'm ambitious. I want to get ahead in this company, and I want to get up to the policy-making level. Money is a part of it, I suppose, but big money comes along naturally with big responsibility, and so I don't worry about that. When you are at the operating level, there is a limit to what you can do, and I have a lot of ideas. I want to get up to where I will be head, and where I can really make a contribution. I don't want just to carry out somebody else's ideas, and you have to be in a top spot if you want to be creative and to get your ideas accepted.

If a man has any ability at all, the older and more experienced he gets, the wiser he becomes, and the better is his judgment. So he would be wasted on low level jobs, and in fact he would be bored with them because he wouldn't be working up to his capabilities. This means that if you want to stay alert and get any satisfaction at all from your work, you have to keep moving up in the organization so that you are faced with bigger and bigger problems, and more and more challenges. That's why I want to move up the ladder, and if I can't in this company, I'll go to another one where I can.

This company almost never terminates a man who is in the first or second levels of management, especially if he has any tenure at all. It's only at the higher levels that anyone actually notices you. So a lot of fellows are happy to make a career at the bottom, because there they have security. But I want action, and if I have to take some risks to get it that's OK. by me. I've only got one life to live, and I want it to be a full and exciting one. I think I'm as good as the next guy, and maybe even a little

bit better. So I see no reason for not aiming high. I'm sure
I can cut it, and I'm sure I'll have a lot of fun doing it.

FINE

The talented manager is a leader and a good one. While he
is reserved in his relationships with his subordinates, he is by no
means an autocrat. He has the intellectual power to deal with highly
complex problems, and is original in his thinking. Therefore, he is
fully justified in being confident in his abilities. He is decisive in
his actions, and his efforts are both forceful and directed. He seeks
self-fulfillment in doing work which is of significance. Thus is the
result of our exploration of managerial talent. Admittedly, our exploration has been incomplete, and very likely it contains inaccuracies.
Certainly some of our descriptions are exaggerations, but by overem-
phasizing the features of a map its topography is thereby clarified,
and let us hope that this is the case here.

As the technology of our industrial society continues to become
more and more intricate, the increase in its managerial requirements
is even greater. Therefore, it is imperative that we understand the
nature of managerial talent so as to utilize it more effectively in the
increasingly complicated government of our organizations.

It is quite possible, if not actually probable, that at the lowest
levels of management the potentialities of those persons who possess
a high degree of managerial talent go unrecognized. Indeed, men
and women with such talent often are misjudged as being poorly
endowed for executive and administrative careers. The jobs at the
lower levels in an organization ordinarily are routine, and higher
management expects them to be kept routine, presuming thus to
assure the uninterrupted functioning of the firm's operation. Originality and creativity are neither needed nor desired. Individuality is
regarded as a disturber of the order of things. By the very nature
of the situation intellectual challenges just do not exist. Very likely,
supervision is simply the handing on of directives originating from
above rather than true leadership designed to utilize fully the potentialities of subordinates. Responsibility, if there is any at all, is very
minimal.

As a consequence, the young man of talent will almost certainly find no outlet for his special qualities in beginning management jobs. Indeed, should he attempt to exercise them he will be behaving in ways counter to those prescribed by the firm. He is in much the same position as the precocious child in the elementary grades of school. The tasks he is assigned are so simple that they do not challenge him, and as a consequence, are boring and therefore poorly done. Any attempt on his part to utilize his high level of ability makes his behavior so unique that he is regarded as peculiar and maladjusted, rather than as gifted. The talented manager who by virtue of his very talent seeks self-realization in significant activities is thus defeated by the system, and is regarded as being unsuitable managerial material.

It is no wonder, then, that at the beginning of their managerial careers so many superior young men move from firm to firm. They find that the descriptions of their firms as given by recruiters and personnel officers to be at variance with the actual facts of the situation when they enter those firms. They must move about until through first-hand experience they find a firm that really wants to utilize their talents and provides circumstances wherein they can be exercised.

The lower level management jobs, then, often do not permit superior managerial talent to manifest itself, and, in fact, may inhibit its manifestation. Therefore, a thoughtful and planful firm must necessarily provide itself with a machinery for the early identification of true managerial talent among its young people, and foster it in the early years by some appropriately designed program involving challenge and responsibility. Furthermore, there must be a system of career planning to insure the advancement of those with high managerial talent to the higher levels of the organization, for under ordinary circumstances those young men who survive the first few years in managerial positions either were mediocre and less creative when they came to the firm, or have had their managerial talent beaten out of them. Managerial talent must be deliberately searched for and fostered, for the normal static nature and bureaucracy of the organization prevents its manifestation.

TABLES

TABLE 1

Intercorrelations Among the Scores Earned by the Sample of the General Population on the Various Scales

	Int	Ini	SAs	Dec	MF	WCA	Mat	Ach	SAc	Pow	Fin	Sec
Sup	.25	.35	.37	.38	-.25	-.15	.05	.33	.34	-.11	-.22	-.43
Int		.28	.45	.15	-.19	-.14	-.13	.63	.26	.10	.12	-.22
Ini			.55	.27	.11	-.01	.32	.53	.39	.09	-.30	-.31
SAs				.39	.11	-.06	.16	.50	.39	.08	-.30	-.31
Dec					-.17	-.15	-.03	.30	.35	.05	-.20	-.26
MF						.23	.37	.02	.02	.06	-.32	.18
WCA							.26	-.07	-.09	.07	-.27	.21
Mat								.23	-.04	.00	-.60	.11
Ach									.32	.02	-.29	-.44
SAc										-.01	-.20	-.47
Pow											.15	-.11
Fin												.08
Sec												

129

TABLE 2

Intercorrelations Among the Scores Earned by the Sample of Managers on the Various Scales

	Int	Ini	SAs	Dec	MF	WCA	Mat	Ach	SAc	Pow	Fin	Sec
Sup	.36	.35	.29	.45	-.10	-.31	-.11	.52	.37	-.04	-.18	-.52
Int		.30	.40	.24	-.12	-.23	-.13	.59	.42	.03	.03	-.33
Ini			.43	.41	.20	-.20	.18	.59	.44	.11	-.51	-.35
SAs				.42	.18	-.04	.02	.47	.35	.19	-.19	-.25
Dec					.00	-.17	-.14	.52	.37	.12	-.29	-.39
MF						.09	.32	.13	.02	.16	-.33	.04
WCA							.12	-.16	-.01	-.14	-.05	.21
Mat								.12	-.11	.07	-.38	.16
Ach									.43	.02	-.41	-.54
SAc										.04	-.21	-.62
Pow											.16	-.08
Fin												.18
Sec												

TABLE 3

Scores on the Supervisory Scale of Persons Assigned Supervisory Functions and Those Not Assigned Such Functions in Three Different Occupational Groups

Mean	Standard Deviation	Number	Group
32.3	13.5	136	Executive management
28.7	13.5	155	Staff management
31.9	10.2	54	Office supervisors
27.8	12.0	98	Clerical workers
27.3	15.9	159	Foremen
25.0	8.2	174	Industrial workers

TABLE 4

Scores on the Supervisory Scale of Persons at Different Levels of Management

Mean	Standard Deviation	Number	Group
31.1	5.8	113	Top management
28.8	6.3	176	Middle management
26.8	6.0	172	Lower management

TABLE 5

Coefficients of Correlation Between Scores on the Supervisory Scale and Job Success of Various Groups of Workers

Coefficient of Correlation	Number	Group
		Managers
.35	89	District managers, insurance company
.65	21	Personnel officers, insurance company
.75	20	Managers, food processing plant
.52	22	Managers, chemical plant
.55		Average
		Line Supervisors
.48	40	Office managers
.12	25	Office managers
.32	63	Foreman, oil refinery
.49	24	Foremen, metal plant
.37		Average
		Line Workers
.51	14	Skilled machine operators
.00	42	Office workers
−.05	64	Skilled workers, metal plant
.06	32	Unskilled workers, metal plant
.13		Average

TABLE 6

Coefficients of Correlation Between Scores on the Intelligence Scale and Scores on Other Intelligence Tests

Coefficient of Correlation	Test	Number	Group
.60	Analysis of Relationships	20	Employed persons
.58	Analysis of Relationships	43	University students
.52	Otis Employment Test	148	Employed persons

TABLE 7

Coefficients of Correlation Between Scores on the Intelligence Scale and the Job Success of Persons at Different Occupational Levels

Coefficient of Correlation	Number	Group
		Managers
.45	21	Personnel officers, insurance company
.34	25	Office managers
.28	89	District managers, insurance company
.07	20	Line managers, food packing plant
.01	22	Line managers, chemical plant
.23		Average
		Line Supervisors
.34	25	Supervising clerks
.25	24	Supervising clerks
.05	24	Foreman, metal plant
−.11	63	Foremen, oil refinery
.13		Average
		Clerical Personnel
.20	42	Office workers
		Industrial Workers
.43	14	Skilled machine operators
−.10	64	Skilled workers, metal plant
−.24	32	Unskilled workers, metal plant
.03		Average

TABLE 8

Means and Standard Deviations of Scores on the Intelligence Scale of Persons at Different Occupational Levels

Mean	Standard Deviation	Number	Group
43.1	6.7	118	Upper management
40.9	7.5	230	Middle management
41.8	6.1	126	Salesmen
38.5	7.8	113	Office workers
34.8	7.8	152	Line supervisors
34.6	7.3	82	Skilled workers
32.8	6.5	68	Semiskilled workers
31.8	5.6	33	Unskilled workers

TABLE 9

Means and Standard Deviations of Scores on the Initiative Scale of Persons in Different Occupational Groups

Mean	Standard Deviation	Number	Group
33.2	5.8	110	Top management personnel
30.9	7.3	80	Middle management personnel
30.2	7.6	42	Supervising and higher clerks
29.4	6.7	146	Foremen
28.9	6.1	61	Routine clerks
27.2	6.3	169	Industrial workers

TABLE 10

The Means and Standard Deviations of Scores on the Self-Assurance Scale earned by Persons at Different Levels of Management

Mean	Standard Deviation	Number	Group
28.6	4.5	113	Top management
26.7	5.3	176	Middle management
24.9	5.1	172	Line management

TABLE 11

The Means and Standard Deviations of Scores on the Decisiveness Scale of Scores Earned by Different Occupational Groups

Mean	Standard Deviation	Number	Group
23.4	3.9	34	"Hard sell" salesmen
21.6	4.6	45	"Soft sell" salesmen
23.4	4.8	135	Line management
19.6	4.4	91	Staff management

TABLE 12

The Means and Standard Deviations of Scores on the Working Class Affinity Scale of Mechanical Workers Differing in the Number of Sociometric Popularity Votes They Received

Mean	Standard Deviation	Number	Sociometric Popularity Votes
17.1	3.6	42	High
16.7	3.3	60	Medium
15.3	3.5	55	Low

TABLE 13

Scores on the Occupational Achievement Scale of Persons in Various Occupations

Mean	Standard Deviation	Number	Occupation
44.8	24.8	57	Professional personnel
44.8	13.5	113	Upper management personnel
40.9	18.1	177	Middle management personnel
33.5	17.8	102	Clerical workers
33.1	22.5	157	Foremen
30.0	18.5	64	Skilled workers
27.1	18.4	69	Semiskilled workers
24.3	18.2	34	Unskilled workers

TABLE 14

The Coefficients of Correlation Between Scores on the Occupational Achievement Scale and Job Success for Persons in Jobs at Different Occupational Levels

Coefficient of Correlation	Number	Group
		Management
.36	89	District managers, insurance company
.46	21	Personnel officers, insurance company
.11	25	Office managers
.04	20	Managers, food processing plant
.24	22	Managers, chemical plant
.24		Average
		Line Supervisors
−.04	63	Foremen, oil refinery
−.09	24	Foremen, metal plant
−.07		Average
		Line Workers
−.08	14	Skilled machine operators
.06	42	Office workers
.06	64	Skilled workers, metal plant
−.35	32	Unskilled workers, metal plant
−.08		Average

APPENDICES

APPENDIX 1
THE SELF-DESCRIPTION INVENTORY

The purpose of this inventory is to obtain a picture of the traits you believe you possess, and to see how you describe yourself. There are no right or wrong answers, so try to describe yourself as accurately and honestly as you can.

In each of the pairs of words below, check the one you think *most* describes you.

1. ___capable
   ___discreet

2. ___understanding
   ___thorough

3. ___cooperative
   ___inventive

4. ___friendly
   ___cheerful

5. ___energetic
   ___ambitious

6. ___persevering
   ___independent

7. ___loyal
   ___dependable

8. ___determined
   ___courageous

9. ___industrious
   ___practical

10. ___planful
    ___resourceful

11. ___unaffected
    ___alert

12. ___sharp-witted
    ___deliberate

13. ___kind
    ___jolly

14. ___efficient
    ___clear-thinking

15. ___realistic
    ___tactful

16. ___enterprising
    ___intelligent

17. ___affectionate
    ___frank

18. ___progressive
    ___thrifty

19. ___sincere
    ___calm

20. ___thoughtful
    ___fair-minded

21.____poised
____ingenious

22.____sociable
____steady

23.____appreciative
____good-natured

24.____pleasant
____modest

25.____responsible
____reliable

26.____dignified
____civilized

27.____imaginative
____self-controlled

28.____conscientious
____quick

29.____logical
____adaptable

30.____sympathetic
____patient

31.____stable
____foresighted

32.____honest
____generous

In each of the pairs of words below, check the one you think *least* describes you.

33.____shy
____lazy

34.____unambitious
____reckless

35.____noisy
____arrogant

36.____emotional
____headstrong

37.____immature
____quarrelsome

38.____unfriendly
____self-seeking

39.____affected
____moody

40.____stubborn
____cold

41.____conceited
____infantile

42.____shallow
____stingy

43.____unstable
____frivolous

44.____defensive
____touchy

45.____tense
____irritable

46.____dreamy
____dependent

47.____changeable
____prudish

48.____nervous
____intolerant

49.___careless
___foolish

50.___apathetic
___egotistical

51.___despondent
___evasive

52.___distractible
___complaining

53.___weak
___selfish

54.___rude
___self-centered

55.___rattle-brained
___disorderly

56.___fussy
___submissive

57.___opinionated
___pessimistic

58.___shiftless
___bitter

59.___hard-hearted
___self-pitying

60.___cynical
___aggressive

61.___dissatisfied
___outspoken

62.___undependable
___resentful

63.___sly
___excitable

64.___irresponsible
___impatient

APPENDIX 2
THE SCORING KEYS

The following lists give the correct responses for each of the various scales. The first number is the item number and the last number is the weight or score of the item. T means the top adjective of the pair is the correct response, and B means the bottom adjective is correct.

Supervisory Ability	Intelligence		Initiative	Self-Assurance	Decisiveness
4 B2	3 B4	59 T1	3 B3	2 B2	1 T2
5 T2	4 B2	60 B1	9 T2	7 B1	8 T1
14 B3	8 T2	61 B1	11 B3	11 B1	9 T2
15 B3	9 B1	62 T1	12 B2	12 T2	10 B1
21 T2	10 B2	64 T2	17 B3	13 T1	12 T2
23 T3	12 T2		19 B2	16 B2	16 T2
25 T3	13 T2		21 B3	18 T2	19 T2
27 T3	16 B4		25 T5	20 T1	22 T2
30 T2	19 B2		32 T2	22 B1	24 T2
31 B3	22 B1		33 B3	24 T2	26 T2
33 B1	24 T1		35 B3	25 T2	30 T1
34 T2	25 T3		47 B3	26 T1	34 T3
35 T4	27 T1		53 T3	27 B1	38 T1
36 B1	34 B1		57 B2	30 B1	42 B1
41 T3	35 B1		59 B3	31 B2	45 B1
42 T2	37 B2		60 T5	33 B2	50 T2
44 B1	39 T2		61 T4	37 T1	53 T1
49 B2	40 B2			38 B1	57 T1
50 T2	41 B4			41 B2	60 T2
51 T2	42 T2			42 B1	61 T2
54 T1	43 T1			43 T2	63 T1
56 B3	45 T1			46 T1	
60 T2	46 B3			50 T2	
61 T2	47 B1			51 T2	
	48 B2			53 T2	
	50 T3			56 B1	
	52 B1			57 T1	
	53 T2			58 T1	
	54 T3			59 B2	
	55 T4			60 T2	
	58 T2			62 T1	

Masculinity-Femininity	Maturity	Working Class Affinity	Achievement Motivation	Need for Self-Actualization
5 B1	1 B1	2 B2	1 B1	3 B2
6 T2	2 B3	4 B1	2 B3	8 T2
11 B1	6 T4	9 T2	3 B3	11 B1
12 B1	8 B1	12 T1	6 T4	12 T2
18 T1	10 B2	13 B2	7 T2	14 B2
23 B2	12 B2	21 T1	20 B4	21 B2
24 B1	13 T1	25 B2	25 T3	26 T1
29 T1	15 B1	31 T2	26 T3	33 B2
30 B1	16 T2	34 B2	27 T3	36 T1
32 T1	18 T1	42 B1	32 B3	49 B1
33 B1	20 B4	43 T1	41 B5	56 B1
34 B1	21 T1	44 B2	47 B2	60 T1
36 B1	22 B4	45 B2	49 B4	
38 T1	28 T1	52 T2	50 T3	
39 B1	33 B1	54 T2	53 T6	
40 T1	34 B1	60 T2	55 T6	
46 B1	35 B3	63 B2	59 B4	
48 T1	37 B1		61 T2	
52 B1	38 B3		63 T3	
55 T1	40 T3		64 T2	
59 B1	43 T1			
60 T1	46 T2			
64 T1	48 B3			
	59 B1			
	60 T4			
	61 T2			
	63 T2			

Need for Power	Need for High Financial Reward	Need for Security
7 T1	6 B1	3 T2
12 B1	13 T1	7 B1
18 T1	16 B1	8 T1
20 B1	22 T1	11 T2
24 T1	29 T1	12 B1
30 B1	57 T1	14 T1
33 B1	59 T1	18 B1
34 T1	60 B3	20 T1
35 B2		21 T1
37 T1		27 B3
42 T1		31 T2
48 T1		36 B1
51 T1		37 B2
58 T1		45 T1
59 T2		49 T1
63 B2		53 B1
64 T1		57 T1

APPENDIX 3
NORMS

Supervisory Ability		Intelligence		Initiative		Self-Assurance	
Score	Percentile Rank	Score	Percentile Rank	Score	Percentile Rank	Score	Percentile Rank
43	99	56	99	47	99	39	99
42	98	55	98	46	98	38	98
41	97	54	97	45	97	37	96
40	93	53	96	44	96	36	94
39	89	52	93	43	95	35	91
38	85	51	90	42	92	34	87
37	80	50	86	41	90	33	82
36	76	49	82	40	87	32	74
35	72	48	77	39	83	31	65
34	67	47	72	38	77	30	56
33	61	46	67	37	71	29	47
32	55	45	62	36	63	28	39
31	48	44	57	35	56	27	33
30	43	43	53	34	50	26	27
29	37	42	49	33	44	25	22
28	32	41	44	32	38	24	18
27	28	40	40	31	33	23	14
26	23	39	35	30	28	22	9
25	19	38	30	29	22	21	7
24	15	37	26	28	18	20	6
23	9	36	22	27	14	19	5
22	8	35	19	26	13	18	4
21	6	34	16	25	10	17	3
20	5	33	14	24	8	16	2
19	3	32	12	23	6	15	1
18	2	31	10	22	5		
17	1	30	8	21	4		
		29	6	20	3		
		28	5	19	2		
		27	4	18	1		
		26	3				
		25	2				
		24	1				

Decisiveness		Masculinity-Femininity		Maturity		Working Class Affinity	
Score	Percentile Rank	Score	Percentile Rank	Score	Percentile Rank	Score	Percentile Rank
32	99	21	99	46	99	23	99
31	97	20	96	45	98	22	98
30	95	19	91	44	97	21	97
29	90	18	82	43	96	20	94
28	85	17	68	42	95	19	89
27	79	16	54	41	94	18	82
26	72	15	37	40	92	17	75
25	65	14	20	39	89	16	64
24	59	13	11	38	86	15	48
23	50	12	6	37	82	14	37
22	41	11	3	36	76	13	27
21	34	10	2	35	69	12	20
20	28	9	1	34	62	11	12
19	22			33	55	10	7
18	15			32	49	9	3
17	12			31	42	8	1
16	9			30	35		
15	6			29	29		
14	4			28	23		
13	3			27	18		
12	2			26	14		
11	1			25	10		
				24	7		
				23	6		
				22	5		
				21	4		
				20	3		
				19	2		
				18	1		

Achievement Motivation		Need for Self-Actualization		Need for Power		Need for High Financial Reward	
Score	Percentile Rank	Score	Percentile Rank	Score	Percentile Rank	Score	Percentile Rank
58	99	17	99	16	99	10	99
57	98	16	98	15	96	9	98
56	97	15	94	14	88	8	95
55	96	14	87	13	78	7	89
54	94	13	78	12	66	6	70
53	91	12	68	11	42	5	65
52	88	11	54	10	26	4	42
51	84	10	34	9	14	3	21
50	81	9	20	8	8	2	6
49	77	8	11	7	3	1	1
48	73	7	4	6	1		
47	69	6	2				
46	64	5	1				
45	60						
44	56						
43	51					Need for Security	
42	46					Score	Percentile Rank
41	39					19	99
40	35					18	98
39	30					17	97
38	26					16	94
37	23					15	87
36	21					14	78
35	19					13	68
34	17					12	61
33	15					11	52
32	13					10	44
31	12					9	37
30	10					8	26
29	9					7	17
28	7					6	10
27	5					5	5
26	4					4	1
25	3						
24	2						
23	1						

APPENDIX 4
MEANS AND STANDARD DEVIATIONS OF SCORES
ON THE VARIOUS SCALES

General Employed Population		Managers		
Mean	Standard Deviation	Mean	Standard Deviation	
26.91	6.46	30.46	6.26	Supervisory ability
37.14	7.93	41.61	7.57	Intelligence
38.71	6.69	32.86	6.40	Initiative
24.36	4.75	28.30	5.85	Self-assurance
19.04	4.74	22.23	4.85	Decisiveness
14.22	3.22	15.31	2.39	Masculinity-femininity
14.73	3.40	14.49	3.28	Working class affinity
29.82	6.38	31.63	5.83	Maturity
33.07	9.95	41.81	8.65	Achievement motivation
9.18	2.58	10.50	2.50	Need for self-actualization
10.34	2.12	10.80	2.17	Need for power over others
5.03	2.02	4.05	1.85	Need for high financial reward
12.44	3.64	10.26	3.61	Need for job security

APPENDIX 5
MEANS AND STANDARD DEVIATIONS OF THE SCORES OF MANAGERS, SUPERVISORS, AND WORKERS ON THE VARIOUS SCALES

	Mean			Standard Deviation		
	Managers	Supervisors	Workers	Managers	Supervisors	Workers
Supervisory ability	30.46	27.04	26.65	6.26	6.42	4.45
Intelligence	41.61	35.41	35.14	7.57	7.90	8.83
Initiative	32.86	29.46	28.16	6.39	7.02	6.29
Self-assurance	28.30	25.11	24.41	5.85	5.47	4.43
Decisiveness	22.23	18.67	18.60	4.85	4.58	4.40
Masculinity-femininity	15.31	15.17	14.91	2.39	3.11	5.59
Maturity	51.56	52.58	47.26	9.07	10.05	10.90
Working class affinity	14.49	15.32	14.87	3.28	3.02	3.33
Need for occupational achievement	41.81	33.75	30.51	8.64	10.30	7.25
Need for self-actualization	10.50	9.46	8.86	2.50	2.84	2.26
Need for power over others	10.80	10.48	10.41	2.17	2.69	2.30
Need for high financial reward	4.05	4.52	5.03	1.85	1.81	2.27
Need for job security	10.26	11.50	12.56	3.61	3.46	3.35

APPENDIX 6
COEFFICIENTS OF CORRELATION BETWEEN THE
SCORES OF MANAGERS, SUPERVISORS, AND WORKERS
ON THE VARIOUS SCALES AND THEIR JOB SUCCESS

	Managers	Supervisors	Workers
Supervisory ability	.46	.34	.10
Intelligence	.27	.06	.03
Initiative	.15	−.07	.02
Self-assurance	.19	.18	−.03
Decisiveness	.22	.15	.05
Masculinity-femininity	−.05	−.07	−.09
Maturity	−.03	.13	.02
Working class affinity	−.17	.07	−.03
Need for occupational achievement	.34	.08	.01
Need for self-actualization	.26	−.03	.05
Need for power over others	.03	.12	−.16
Need for high financial reward	−.18	−.05	−.10
Need for job security	−.30	−.05	−.11

APPENDIX 7
CHART FOR TRANSMUTING RAW SCORES ON THE
MATURITY SCALE TO RELATIVE MATURITY SCORES

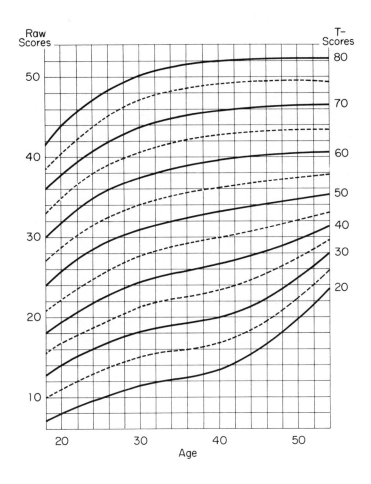

FIGURES

FIGURE 1. Average scores of managers, supervisors, and workers on the measures of abilities.

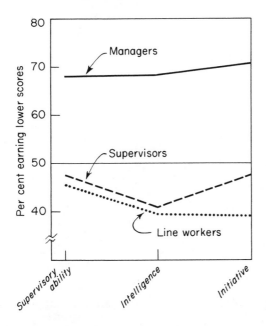

FIGURE 2. Relationships between the scores of managers on the measures of ability and their job success.

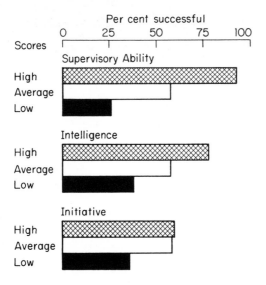

155

FIGURE 3. Coefficients of correlation between the scores of managers, supervisors, and workers on the measures of ability and their job success.

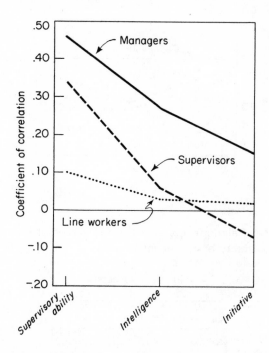

FIGURE 4. The relationship between initiative, age, and occupation.

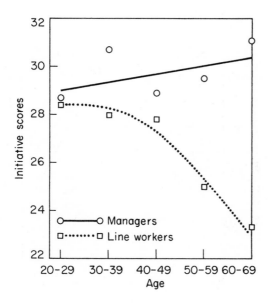

FIGURE 5. Average scores of managers, supervisors, and workers on the measures of personality traits.

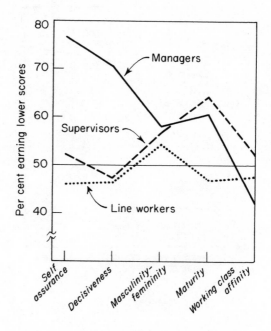

FIGURE 6.   Relationships between the scores of managers on the measures of personality traits and their job success.

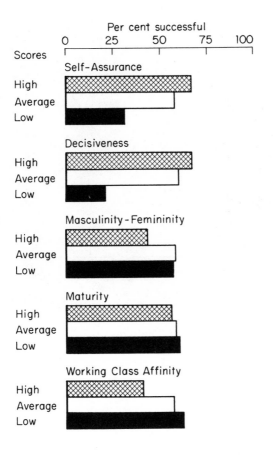

FIGURE 7. Coefficients of correlation between the scores of managers, supervisors, and workers on the measures of personality traits and their job success.

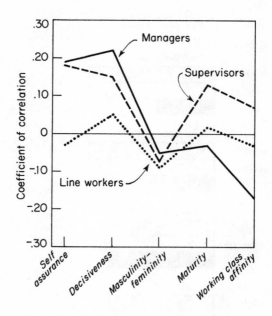

FIGURE 8. The relationship between maturity scores and age.

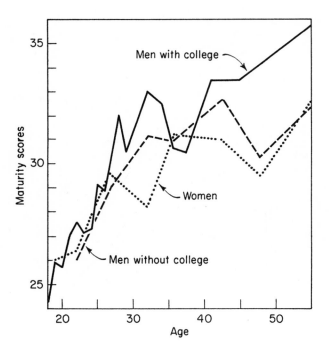

FIGURE 9. Average scores of managers, supervisors, and workers on the measures of motivation.

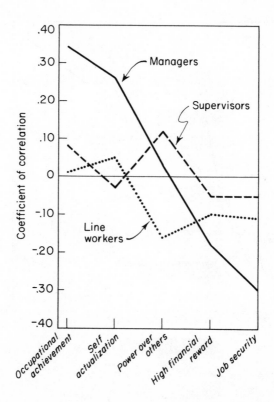

FIGURE 10. Relationships between the scores of managers on the measures of motivation and their job success.

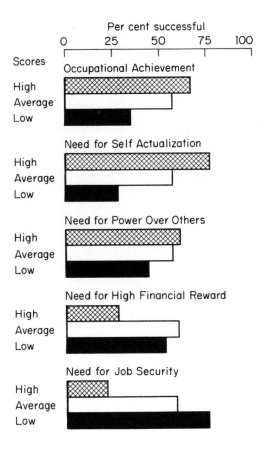

FIGURE 11. Coefficients of correlation between the scores of managers, supervisors, and workers on the measures of motivation and their job success.

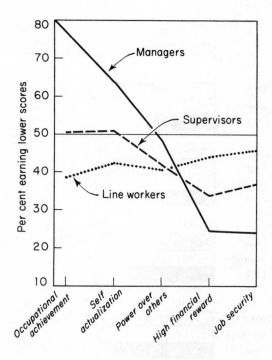

FIGURE 12. The relative importance of the thirteen traits to managerial talent.

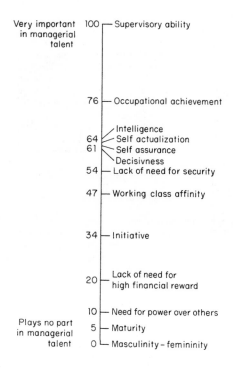

FIGURE 13. The relationship between managerial talent and success in management in one firm.

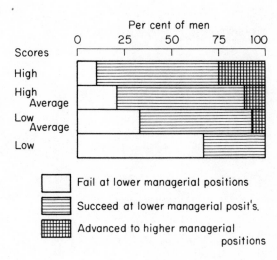